EXPERIMENTS FOR FUTURE
DOCTORS

ROBERT GARDNER
AND JOSHUA CONKLIN

Enslow Publishing
101 W. 23rd Street
Suite 240
New York, NY 10011
USA

enslow.com

Published in 2017 by Enslow Publishing, LLC.
101 W. 23rd Street, Suite 240, New York, NY 10011

Library of Congress Cataloging-in-Publication Data

Names: Gardner, Robert, 1929– author. | Conklin, Joshua, author.
Title: Experiments for future doctors / Robert Gardner and Joshua Conklin.
Description: New York, NY : Enslow Publishing, 2017. | "2017 | Series: Experiments for
   future STEM professionals | Includes bibliographical references and index.
Identifiers: LCCN 2016001574 | ISBN 9780766078543 (library bound)
Subjects: LCSH: Medicine—Experiments—Juvenile literature. | Anatomy—Experiments—
   Juvenile literature. | Science—Experiments—Juvenile literature. | Science projects—Juvenile
   literature.
Classification: LCC QM27 .G37 2017 | DDC 610.78—dc23
LC record available at http://lccn.loc.gov/2016001574

Printed in the United States of America

To Our Readers: We have done our best to make sure all website addresses in this book were active and appropriate when we went to press. However, the author and the publisher have no control over and assume no liability for the material available on those websites or on any websites they may link to. Any comments or suggestions can be sent by e-mail to customerservice@enslow.com.

Photo Credits: Cover, OJO_Images/OJO Images/Getty Images (doctor), Fuse/Getty Images (hospital bed background throughout book), Titov Nikolai/Shutterstock.com (DNA symbol), elic/Shutterstock.com (green geometric background throughout book), Zffoto/Shutterstock.com (white textured background throughout book); p. 48, Hein Nouwens/Shutterstock.com; p. 56, stihii/Shutterstock.com.

Illustrations by Joseph Hill.

CONTENTS

INTRODUCTION

Do you enjoy learning about the human body? Do you have good people skills and enjoy making people feel well? Perhaps you should consider becoming a physician! Although the path to a medical degree (MD or DO) can be long and demanding, it is an exciting career choice for people who love medicine and physiology.

The rewarding career of a doctor begins very early on, requiring many steps and planning. After graduating from high school and college with high grades, you will need to apply to and be accepted by a medical school. To be admitted to a medical school, you must obtain high scores on the Medical College Admissions Test (MCAT) and have good interviews with admissions officers. When you are accepted to a medical school, your first day will likely involve taking the Hippocratic oath, by which you swear to uphold the principles of good medical procedures.

In your first two years of medical school, you will study biochemistry, anatomy, genetics, and other courses involving problem solving, teamwork, communication skills, professionalism, and a commitment to lifelong learning. You will further be asked to handle a lot of facts and practice your skills with critical thinking, colleague unity, formulating medical histories, and doing physical examinations on patients.

During your third and fourth years of medical school, you will begin to apply what you have learned in supervised experiences with real patients. You will also be required to take and pass the United States Medical Licensing Examination (USMLE) before practicing medicine in the United States or Canada.

Some future physicians decide to get both an MD (medical doctor) or DO (doctor of osteopathy) and a PhD in some field related to medicine. Such a path takes seven to eight years. It involves research, teaching, and practicing medicine under supervision.

After medical school, a residency is required to develop a specialty. A residency is a step in graduate medical education allowing the resident physician further experience in the medical field. After another three to five years, you can be certified to practice medicine. Resident physicians learn the specifics of their specialty, teach medical students, and treat patients under the supervision of an attending physician.

The education of a doctor never ends. Physicians are required to continue medical education by enrolling in courses for a certain number of hours every year in order to keep pace with medical innovations and discoveries. While the path is long, the reward of helping people stay healthy and finding ways to treat patients in need is worth it for most doctors.

The cost of a medical education is not cheap! Medical school tuition and living expenses cost approximately $90,000 per year. Although there are scholarships and financial aid available, you can plan on having significant debt by the time you actually begin to practice the profession. Because doctors are well compensated, you should be able to pay off your debts if you plan wisely.

For those who pursue a specialized field of medicine (graduate medical education), funds are often available through the federal government's Medicare program.

WHAT DO DOCTORS DO?

Doctors examine and treat patients in a wide variety of ways. Primary care doctors will treat most common health issues and perform an annual physical examination on each patient to be certain the patient is in good health. If they find anything wrong, they may prescribe a medicine or suggest a cure or a preventative measure, such as exercise or a change in diet. For something more specific, they will probably recommend the patient see a specialist who has the knowledge to better treat the particular need.

The following are brief descriptions of different types of possible careers as a doctor with a medical specialty. You should be aware, too, that people other than medical physicians provide medical services. You have probably been treated by a dentist, a medical professional who has spent four years in a dental school and passed a state board examination. Others involved in medical care include nurses, pharmacists, clinical psychologists, physical therapists, physician's assistants (PAs), and nurse practitioners (NPs). All these occupations provide opportunities in a medical career that you might find rewarding. The experiments in this book are also worthwhile for someone interested in such professions.

TYPES OF DOCTORS

Primary Care physicians provide care and treatment for most common health problems. These doctors are in great demand and provide care to a large number of patients.

Specialists are doctors who focus on a specific illness, tissue, or organ. All have a medical degree—MD or DO—but concentrate on one aspect of medicine. Some of these specialties include:

- **Allergy and immunology** doctors treat allergies and problems involving the immune system.
- **Anesthesiologists** give medications to prevent pain or to make patients unconscious during surgical procedures.
- **Cardiologists** treat patients who have problems with their heart or blood vessels.
- **Dermatologists** specialize in skin diseases such as skin cancer, acne, or psoriasis. They also help patients with problems involving nails or hair.

- **Ear, nose, and throat** physicians treat diseases and problems associated with these areas of the body.
- **Endocrinologists** see patients whose endocrine glands are not functioning properly. A common disease they treat is diabetes.
- **Gastroenterologists** focus on problems related to the digestive tract—esophagus, stomach, intestines, and gall bladder. They do procedures called endoscopies, in which they use lighted tubes to examine tissues all the way from the throat to the rectum.
- **Hematologists** are concerned with blood diseases and blood formation. Their scope of work includes bone marrow, where red blood cells are made.
- **Internal medicine** is the specialty of many primary care doctors. They seek to diagnose and treat adult diseases that do not require surgery.
- **Nephrologists** specialize in the diagnosis and treatment of diseases and abnormalities involving the kidneys.
- **Neurologists** deal with diseases and abnormalities involving the brain, spinal cord, and nerves.
- **Obstetrics and gynecology** is the specialty of doctors who treat female reproductive system conditions, monitor pregnancies, and deliver babies.
- **Oncologists** diagnose and treat cancer and tumors, both benign and malignant.
- **Ophthalmologists** are doctors who treat vision and eye problems.

- **Orthopedic surgeons** are physicians who treat issues with muscles, bones, tendons, and joints. They perform surgeries such as knee and hip replacements.
- **Pathologists** carry out examinations and diagnoses of organs, tissues, and body fluids. They are often called upon to analyze tissues and organs involved in criminal acts.
- **Pediatricians** are doctors who treat children from birth to adolescence.
- **Psychiatrists** treat people who have mental illnesses.
- **Pulmonary physicians** deal with diseases and other issues that affect the lungs and chest tissues.
- **Radiologists** use radiation such as X-rays and other imaging systems to diagnose and treat diseases.
- **Rheumatologists** are doctors who treat patients with rheumatism and other disorders that reduce a patient's mobility due to changes in muscles, tendons, and bones. A common complaint they encounter is arthritis among aging patients.
- **Surgeons** treat diseases and injuries using operative procedures. A surgeon might remove your tonsils, appendix, or gall bladder.
- **Urologists** are concerned with diseases or problems involving the urinary system and male reproductive organs, especially the prostate.

BEFORE YOU BEGIN EXPERIMENTING: SOME SUGGESTIONS

At times, as you do the experiments in this book, you may need a partner. It would be best to partner with someone who also enjoys experiments and discoveries in order to get the most enjoyment from your work. When doing some of the anatomy experiments, pay attention to how your partner feels. If they ask you to stop, listen to them. Bedside manner is an important part of being a doctor, and it is necessary to act professionally and appropriately to make your patient feel comfortable. **If any safety issues or danger is involved in doing an experiment, you will be warned. In some cases, to avoid danger, you will be asked to work with an adult. Please do so.** We don't want you to take any chances that could lead to an injury and send *you* to a doctor!

Like any good doctor, you will find it useful to record your ideas, notes, data, and conclusions in a notebook. By doing so, you can keep track of the information you gather and the conclusions you reach. It will allow you to refer to things you have done and help you in doing future projects. It may also come in handy during college or job interviews as a point of reference.

THE SCIENTIFIC METHOD

Many doctors are involved in scientific research as they search for cures for various diseases or seek to understand complex diseases or disabilities. They ask questions, make careful observations, and conduct research. Different areas of medicine use different approaches. Depending on the problem, one method is likely to be better than another. Designing a new artificial heart, finding a cure for lung cancer, or constructing an artificial limb require different techniques, but they all demand an understanding of how good science is done.

Despite the differences, all medical scientists use a similar approach to experimenting. It is called the scientific method. In most experiments, some or all of the following steps are used: making an observation, formulating a question, making a hypothesis (one possible answer to the question) and a prediction (an if-then statement), designing and conducting one or more experiments, analyzing the results in order to reach conclusions about your prediction, and the acceptance or rejection of the hypothesis. Medical scientists share their findings. They write articles about their experiments and their results. The writings are reviewed by other scientists before being published in journals for wider circulation.

You might wonder where and how to begin an experiment. Simply observe the world around you with a scientist's curiosity. Your observations may then result in a question, which could arise from an earlier experiment or from reading, and may then be answered by a well-designed investigation. Once you have a question, your job is to make a hypothesis, which is a possible answer to the question (what you think will happen). Once you have a hypothesis, it is time to design an experiment to test a consequence of your hypothesis.

In most cases, it is appropriate to do a controlled experiment. This means having two groups that are treated exactly the same except for the single factor being tested. That factor is called a variable. For example, suppose the question is: "Is medicine X really a cure for disease Y?"

Scientists would establish two groups of patients, both of whom have disease Y. One group would receive medicine X. A second group would unknowingly be given what is known as a placebo—a pill known to have no effect on the disease. If neither group shows any improvement, it is clear that medicine X is not a cure. If the group receiving the medicine is cured of the disease, then the experiment would be ended. The group not receiving the medicine would then be given the medicine so that they, too, could be cured.

Two other terms are often used in scientific experiments—dependent and independent variables. The dependent variable depends on the value of the independent variable. For example, the area of a plot of land depends on the length and width of the plot. Here, the dependent value is the area. It depends on the length and width, which are the independent variables in this example.

After the data is collected, it is analyzed to see if it supports or rejects the hypothesis. If medicine X cures the group that received it, then the data would support the hypothesis that medicine X is a cure for the disease in question.

The results of one experiment can lead to a related question. They may send you in a different direction. Whatever the results, something can be learned from every experiment.

SAFETY FIRST

Safety is imperative in science and medicine. Certain rules apply when conducting experiments. Some of the rules below may seem obvious and others may not, but it is important that they are all followed. Any workplace involving science or medicine will have a similar code of conduct. It is best to start learning how to work like a doctor now.

1. Have an adult help you whenever this book, or any other, so advises.
2. Wear eye protection and closed-toe shoes (not sandals). Tie back long hair.
3. Do not eat or drink while experimenting. Never taste substances being used (unless instructed to do so).
4. Do not touch chemicals with your bare hands. Use tools, such as spatulas, to transfer chemicals from place to place.
5. The liquid in some thermometers is mercury (a dense liquid metal). It is dangerous to touch mercury or breathe mercury vapor. Mercury thermometers have been banned in many states. When

doing experiments that require you to measure temperature, use only electronic or non-mercury thermometers, such as those filled with alcohol. If you have a mercury thermometer in the house, **ask an adult** if it can be taken to a local thermometer exchange location.

6. Do only those experiments that are described in this book or those that have been approved by **an adult**.

7. Maintain a serious attitude while conducting experiments. Never engage in horseplay or play practical jokes while conducting experiments.

8. Before beginning an experiment, read all the instructions carefully and be sure you understand them.

9. Remove all items not needed for the experiment from your work space.

10. At the end of every activity, clean all materials used and put them away. Then wash your hands thoroughly with soap and water.

The chapters that follow contain experiments and information that every future young doctor should know. They can help you decide if medicine is a career you want to pursue.

CHAPTER ONE

TESTS THAT DOCTORS DO

Undoubtedly you've experienced some of the daily tests that doctors and nurses perform. In this chapter, you will get to carry out some of those same tests while learning the science behind them.

EXPERIMENT 1

TAKING A PULSE

Doctors, PAs (physician's assistants), NPs (nurse practitioners), and nurses often check a patient's pulse. It's a quick way to see if a patient's resting heart rate (the heart rate while sitting and resting) is normal—about seventy beats per minute. Well-trained athletes often have a slower resting heart rate.

A rapid or irregular heart rate is easily detected by placing fingers on an artery that passes through everyone's wrist.

Uncommon rates or an irregular beat would raise concern. Some people get nervous when they go to the doctor, and their heart beats faster. The doctor may understand this and take your pulse again at the end of your exam.

When your heart contracts, it forces blood into and along your arteries. Arteries are elastic. They stretch like a rubber band when more blood is pumped into them. The expansion of an artery can be felt if the artery is close to the surface of a person's body. What you can feel is called a pulse because the artery pulsates (throbs) as blood is forced through it by the heart.

1. You can easily take your own pulse. Put your first two fingers on the underside of your opposite arm's wrist just beyond the point where your thumb connects with your wrist. (See Figure 1a.)

    Your pulse rate is the number of pulses you feel per minute, but you don't have to count for a full minute. Just count the number of pulses for fifteen seconds and multiply that count by four; it will give you your heart rate in beats per minute.

2. If you amplify your pulse, you can make it visible. To do so, put your hand, palm upward, on a table.

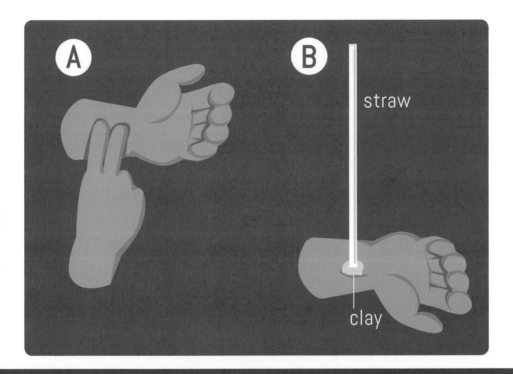

Figure 1. a) A pulse can be felt on the inside of your wrist just behind your thumb. b) With a lump of clay and a soda straw, you can amplify your pulse and make it visible.

Put a small lump of clay on the site of your pulse. Stick a straw upright in the clay as shown in Figure 1b. What happens to the straw each time your heart beats?

3. It might be fun to show a parent or friend how you can amplify their pulse.

4. Arteries are close to the surface at other points in your body. Another pulse, often used by doctors, is found on either side of your larynx (Adam's apple). Can you find that pulse? There's another pulse just in

front of your ear. Can you find it? Can you locate a pulse on the inside of your elbow? How about your ankle?

5. Take a partner's pulse at both his neck and his wrist at the same time. Which pulse do you expect to feel first? Try it! Were you right?

    Your heart is about the size of your fist. It weighs about 290 grams (10.2 ounces). But it is an amazing pump. Each time your heart beats, it pushes about 130 mL (4.4 oz) of blood into your arteries.

6. Try this heart math. Assuming your heart beats seventy times each minute, how many milliliters of blood does it pump in one minute?

    A liter (L) is 1,000 mL. How many liters of blood does it pump each minute? A liter is equal to 1.06 quarts. How many quarts of blood does your heart pump every minute? How many gallons does it pump per minute?

    How many liters of blood does your heart pump each hour? Each day?

EXPLORING ON YOUR OWN

Using an anatomy book, identify the major arteries and veins of the human body. After studying these vessels, where might you expect to find pulses? Can you find them?

YOUR HEART

The human heart, like all mammalian hearts, has four chambers. (See Figure 2.) The two upper chambers are the right and left atria. The lower chambers are the right and left ventricles. Blood returns to the heart from the various parts of the body in veins. The two main veins carrying blood to the right atrium are the superior and inferior vena cava. When the heart muscle contracts, the contraction begins in the atria. The contraction is caused by an electrical signal that starts in the brain and travels through the vagus nerve to the right atrium. The atria contract first, forcing blood through the tricuspid and mitral valves into the right and left ventricles. Soon after the atria contract, the ventricles contract, forcing blood through the pulmonary and aortic valves into the pulmonary artery and the aorta.

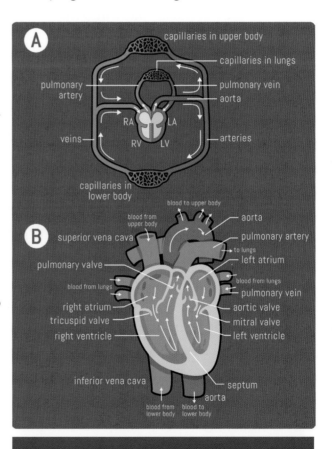

Figure 2. a) This is the general structure of the circulatory system (R = right; L = left; A = atrium; V = ventricle). b) A more detailed look shows the heart and the vessels leading to it (veins) and from it (arteries).

Let's trace a drop of blood as it enters the right atrium. This venous blood has passed close to cells of the body where it has lost much of its oxygen (O_2) while increasing its concentration of carbon dioxide (CO_2). As the heart contracts, the drop of blood, along with other blood, is forced though the tricuspid valve into the right ventricle. As the ventricles contract following the contraction of the atria, the drop is pushed through the pulmonary valve into the pulmonary artery. The pulmonary artery, under pressure from the contracting heart, carries the drop of blood to the lungs. There the artery branches out into smaller arteries that carry blood to all parts of the lung. Eventually the arteries become capillaries. Capillaries are very small vessels with walls so thin that gases dissolved in the blood can pass through them. It is here that the drop of blood picks up oxygen (O_2) from air in the lungs and transfers its CO_2 to the lung air. The oxygenated drop of blood is transported back to the heart through veins. These veins merge to form the pulmonary vein that brings the blood back to the heart's left atrium.

As the heart contracts, blood passes from the left atrium to the left ventricle through the mitral valve. During the next heart contraction, the blood is pushed from the left ventricle through the aortic valve into the aorta, the body's main artery. The aorta branches into smaller arteries and the blood eventually reaches capillaries. In the capillaries, O_2 is transferred to body cells, and CO_2 moves from cells of the body into the blood. The capillaries come together to form veins that carry blood back to the heart's right atrium. Truly, your heart is an amazing organ!

EXPERIMENT 2

LISTENING TO THE HEART

As illustrated by the previous description, your heart does a lot of complicated work. Doctors listen to your heart because all that work causes meaningful noises. By listening to these noises, they can tell whether or not your heart is behaving normally. Abnormal sounds or rhythms could indicate heart

> ### THINGS YOU WILL NEED
>
> - **stethoscope (your family may have one or obtain from medical supply store or science supply house)**
> - **a partner**
> - **clock or watch**

disease or other problems. If you have access to a stethoscope, you can listen to the sounds of the heart.

1. Place the ear buds of a stethoscope into your ears.
2. Put the flat chest piece slightly to the left of the center of your chest. Move the chest piece to slightly different places until you hear the heart sounds clearly and loudly.
3. Listen for two sounds. They occur close together in time. The first sound is longer. The second is a short, sharp sound. Together they sound like "lubb-dup."

The "lubb" is caused by the contracting heart muscle and the closing of the valves between the atria and ventricles. The "dup" is the sound of the aortic and pulmonary valves slamming shut as the heart relaxes after both the atria and ventricles have contracted.

When the heart muscle relaxes, it is no longer pushing the blood. Therefore, the blood tends to flow back into the heart. However, the valves that connect the ventricles to the aorta and pulmonary artery are like the doors to a room. They open only one way—outward, into the aorta and pulmonary artery. When the blood tries to flow back into the heart, the valves slam shut with a loud "dup" sound.

4. If you don't have a stethoscope, you can hear the heart's sounds by placing your ear against the chest of a partner. (Your partner will probably want to hear your heart as well.)

While listening to your heart, count the number of times it beats in fifteen seconds. Does it agree with the count you found when you used your pulse to measure your heart rate—the number of times your heart beats in one minute? What is your heart rate?

EXPLORING ON YOUR OWN

Which do you predict should happen first, hearing the heart beat or feeling a pulse? Design an experiment to test your hypothesis.

EXPERIMENT 3

LISTENING TO THE LUNGS

Doctors use a stethoscope to listen to air moving into the lungs. You can do the same thing.

THINGS YOU WILL NEED

- **stethoscope**
- **a partner or family member**

1. Place a stethoscope on the back of a partner or family member. Then ask that person to take a deep breath.

2. Listen carefully. You should hear the sound of air rushing into a lung. Doctors can place the stethoscope over different lobes of a lung. If air is not reaching a lung as it normally should, the sound will be absent or much less intense. There are other lung sounds that can help a doctor detect a problem.

EXPERIMENT 4

CHECKING A PATIENT'S HEARING

Here is an easy way to test a person's hearing. It won't tell you if a person can't hear certain frequencies (tones), but it will indicate an ability to hear reasonably well or not.

> **THINGS YOU WILL NEED**
>
> • **one or more "patients"**

1. Ask someone to sit quietly in a chair.
2. Stand behind the person and rub your thumb and fingers together to make a soft sound.
3. Ask the "patient" if he or she hears anything. If they do, they pass the hearing test. If they don't hear that sound, suggest they see a hearing specialist.

EXPERIMENT 5

CHECKING THE PATELLAR REFLEX

Doctors often check for problems with the nervous system by seeing if a common reflex, the patellar reflex, is normal. You can easily test the patellar reflex at home.

> ### THINGS YOU WILL NEED
>
> - **a partner**
> - **high table or bench**
> - **a rubber hammer or a large rubber stopper and a pencil or pen**

1. You will need a rubber hammer or a large one or two-hole rubber stopper and a large pencil or pen. If you use the rubber stopper, push a pencil or pen into a hole in the stopper so it can be used like a hammer.
2. Ask a partner to sit on a table or bench that is high enough so his or her feet don't reach the floor.
3. Locate a point just below your partner's patella (knee cap) and hold your fingers on that location. Ask your partner to raise his foot a short distance. You will feel the ligament connecting the thigh (quadriceps) muscle to the lower leg move upward.

4. Ask your partner to relax his or her leg. Then strike that ligament with a moderate force using your rubber hammer. Hitting the ligament should produce a reflex causing the leg to straighten as the quadriceps muscle contracts.

    If nothing happens, you probably missed the ligament. Try again.

EXPERIMENT 6

CHECKING THE PUPIL REFLEX

The colored part of the eye is called the iris. Look into a mirror. The black disc you see at the center of your iris is the pupil (See Figure 3). It is the opening through which light enters your eye. The iris has muscles that can change the size (diameter) of the pupil. Nerve cells from the brain are connected to the muscles of the iris. These muscles can make the pupil larger or smaller. A larger pupil allows more light to enter

THINGS YOU WILL NEED

- **a partner**
- **well lit room**
- **flashlight**
- **T-pin or a large needle**
- **black construction paper**
- **well lit window**

the eye, while a small pupil limits the amount of light entering the eye.

There are also sensory nerve cells in the eye that respond to light intensity. This experiment will allow you to see how the pupil responds to the intensity of light as muscles in the iris contract or relax.

1. Ask a partner to sit in a chair in a well lit room.
2. Ask your partner to keep his or her eyes open. Then watch one of your partner's pupils as you shine a flashlight into one of his or her eyes. What happens?

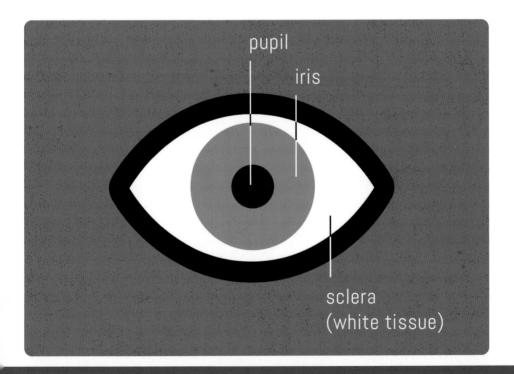

pupil

iris

sclera
(white tissue)

Figure 3. The colored part of your eye is the iris. The black circle, the pupil, at the center of the iris is the opening that allows light to enter the eye.

Do iris muscles in the two eyes respond to light separately or together?

3. To check your answer, ask your partner to cover his or her left eye while you watch the right eye. Does the right pupil shrink when the left eye is covered? Does the left pupil shrink when the right eye is covered? Do iris muscles respond to light separately or together?

4. You can do a similar experiment on yourself. Use a T-pin or a large needle to make a pinhole about 1 mm wide in a small 3 inch (8 cm) square piece of black construction paper. Hold the pinhole close to the pupil of one eye. Turn your other eye toward a well lit window. You will see a circle of light coming through the pinhole in front of your eye.

5. Keep the pinhole in place and cover your other eye. What happens to the size of the circle of light? What happens to the size of the circle when you open the other eye?

6. How can you make the circle shrink and widen in a rhythmic manner?

7. Concentrate on the circle of light. You will see tiny clear dots with dark circles around them, fuzzy lines, or less distinct particles. The particles appear to move slowly across the circle. The things you see are caused by light passing around the tiny particles called floaters. The floaters are in the fluid inside the eye.

A sudden increase of floaters accompanied by flashes of light could indicate a detached retina and should be treated immediately.

EXPLORING ON YOUR OWN

- How are pupils involved in the red eyes sometimes seen in photographs? How can this "red eye" effect be eliminated?
- How can changes in light intensity entering one eye affect the other eye?
- Do pupils respond to stimuli other than light, such as emotions or medication?

MEASURING BLOOD PRESSURE

Has a doctor, PA, NP, or nurse ever measured your blood pressure? If so, you have felt the pressure as air was pumped into the cuff around your upper arm.

When your heart contracts, it pushes more blood into your arteries. This causes the arteries to expand and increases the pressure of the blood pushing against the walls of the arteries.

When a medical person measures your blood pressure, he or she measures both systolic and diastolic pressure. Systolic pressure occurs when the heart contracts, forcing blood into the arteries. Diastolic pressure occurs just before the heart contracts, when pressure in the arteries is at a minimum.

When blood pressure is recorded, the higher or systolic pressure is recorded first followed by the diastolic pressure. A normal blood pressure might be 120/70; that is, 120 mm of mercury for systolic pressure and 70 mm of mercury for diastolic pressure. Like air pressure, blood pressure is measured in millimeters (mm) of mercury. At sea level under normal conditions, Earth's atmospheric pressure, which we measure with a barometer, is 760 mm of mercury. This means the air can support a column of mercury 760 mm (76 cm) or 30 inches high. This is the same pressure as 10.1 newtons per square centimeter or 14.7 pounds per square inch. Of course, blood, like the rest of your body, feels the pressure of the air. Consequently, blood pressure is the pressure by which the blood's pressure exceeds air pressure.

Knowing the systolic and diastolic blood pressure, you can easily calculate what is known as pulse pressure. It is the difference between systolic and diastolic blood pressure. In the example given above, the pulse pressure would be

120 mm – 70 mm = 50 mm of mercury

The pulse you feel in your wrist is due to pulse pressure. It is the amount the blood pressure increases when it causes a pulse that you can feel.

The easiest way to measure blood pressure is with a battery operated monitor that fits over a person's index finger or wrist. It gives a digital display of both systolic and diastolic pressure. Still another battery powered blood pressure monitor inflates at the press of a button. It provides a digital display of blood pressure and pulse rate. Your family may have such an instrument or you may be able to borrow one.

The traditional device for measuring blood pressure is the sphygmomanometer. It is more difficult to operate than the automatic devices. It consists of a cuff that is placed around a person's upper arm. The cuff is inflated when air is pumped into it. The pressure in the cuff is read on a meter. When the pressure in the cuff exceeds the pressure of blood flowing through the brachial artery in the upper arm, the artery collapses. Blood flow through the artery stops.

A valve is used to let air slowly escape from the cuff. As the pressure in the cuff decreases, a point is reached at which systolic pressure allows a spurt of blood to pass through the artery. The short spurt of blood produces a sound. The sound can be heard by placing a stethoscope over the artery below the cuff on the inside of the elbow. When the first sound is heard, the pressure is read on a gauge or manometer attached to the cuff. This is the person's systolic blood pressure.

As more air is released from the cuff, the pressure in the cuff continues to fall. The sound becomes more muffled and eventually disappears. The sound disappears when there is no longer any interference with the flow of blood. At the disappearance of sound, the pressure is again read and recorded as the diastolic blood pressure.

MEASURING THE EFFECT OF BODY POSITION AND EXERCISE ON BLOOD PRESSURE, HEART RATE, AND BREATHING RATE

To measure blood pressure, you should use one of the easier ways, such as a battery-operated monitor that fits over a person's index finger or wrist and gives a digital display of both systolic and diastolic pressure. Or you can use another battery-powered blood pressure monitor that inflates at the press of a button and provides a digital display of blood pressure and pulse rate. Your family may have such an instrument or you may be able to borrow one.

If you use a sphygmomanometer, it should be done under the supervision of an adult who is familiar with the device and has used it many times.

THINGS YOU WILL NEED

- **battery-operated blood pressure monitor**
- **a knowledgeable adult if a sphygmomanometer is used**
- **couch or floor with soft carpet**
- **notebook**
- **pen or pencil**
- **a partner (the subject)**
- **graph paper**

1. Ask a partner to serve as the subject in this experiment. Have him or her lie flat on a couch or soft rug and rest quietly for five minutes.

2. Then, while still lying flat, measure your subject's breathing rate. This is easily done by watching the subject's abdomen. Each up and down movement of the abdomen is one breath. Count breaths for fifteen seconds and multiply by four to obtain the breathing rate per minute. Record the breathing rate in a notebook.

3. Use your subject's wrist pulse to measure his or her heart rate. Record the rate in your notebook.

4. Measure and record your subject's systolic and diastolic blood pressure.

5. Have the subject sit upright for five minutes. After five minutes, again measure and record the subject's breathing rate, pulse rate, and blood pressure.

6. Ask the subject to stand up for five minutes. Again, after five minutes, record the subject's breathing rate, pulse rate, and blood pressure.

7. Finally, have the subject run in place for five minutes.

8. As soon as he or she stops running, measure and record the subject's breathing rate, pulse rate, and blood pressure.

9. Continue to make these measurements at intervals of two to five minutes until pulse rate, breathing rate, and blood pressure return to, or very nearly to, the rates and pressure the subject had before exercising.

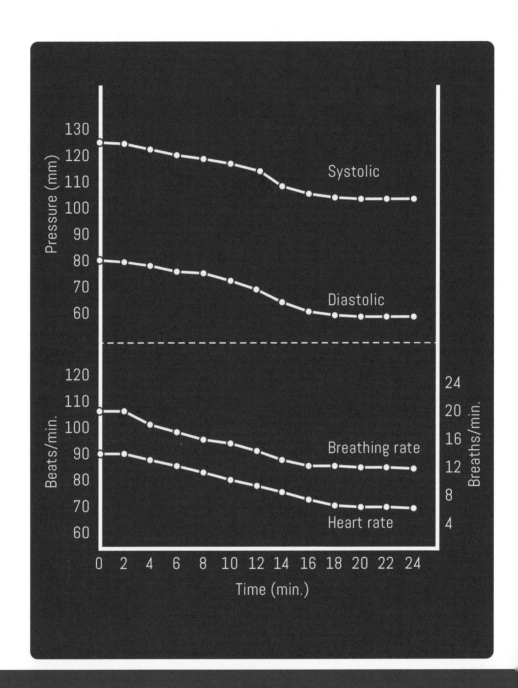

Figure 4. These graphs show blood pressure, breathing rate, and heart rate versus time after exercising. How do these graphs compare with yours?

10. Plot a graph of the subject's breathing rate, pulse rate, and blood pressure versus time, in minutes, for the period following the exercise. It can all be done on one graph similar to the one in Figure 4. What can you conclude from your graph?

EXPLORING ON YOUR OWN

Measure the breathing and heart rates and blood pressures of a number of different people after they have been lying, sitting, standing, and exercising. Does a subject's age or sex seem to affect the results? Is the data different for people who are in good physical condition, such as athletes, versus people who are sedentary or not "in shape"? If so, what are those differences and how can you account for them?

CHAPTER TWO

ANATOMY OF THE HUMAN SKELETON

You are born with 270 bones. By the time you reach adulthood, you have only 206. Your bones don't fall off, but many of them fuse as a human grows from baby to adult.

These bones form what is called your skeleton. A skeleton is the frame on which a body is built. It is much like the steel frame of a skyscraper on which the rest of the building is layered.

The 206 bones that make up the human skeleton can be divided into two main types. One group of bones makes up the axial skeleton. It includes the skull, ribs, sternum, and vertebrae. As the name axial implies, these bones constitute the body's axis—the central line about which the rest of the body is built.

The second group of bones make up the appendicular skeleton. These are the bones of the shoulders, hips, arms, legs, hands, and feet. These bones append (attach) to the axial skeleton.

Bones are connected to other bones and held together at their joints by tough strips of connective tissue called ligaments. The muscles that make bones move are connected to the bones by another type of tough connective tissue called tendons.

Soft bonelike tissue that contains less calcium is called cartilage. This flexible tissue is found in many parts of the body, such as the nose and ears. It is also found at the ends of bones where it cushions the forces between bones in the joints where bones meet.

Every doctor has to be very familiar with the human skeleton and the anatomy connected to it.

EXPERIMENT 8

FINDING THE PARTS OF YOUR SKELETON

You cannot see the bones in your body. They are covered with muscles, connective tissue, and skin. The common names of the body regions covering your bones are shown in Figure 5.

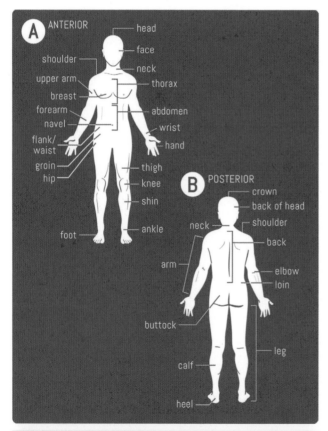

Even though you can't see them, you can feel many of your bones. Your skull, for example, feels like one large bone. Actually, it is a number of separate bones, as shown in Figure 6. But those bones have fused or are fusing.

For example, gaps existed between your skull bones when you were a baby. At birth, human brains are only

Figure 5. These are common names for the various regions of your body. a) Anterior view. b) Posterior view.

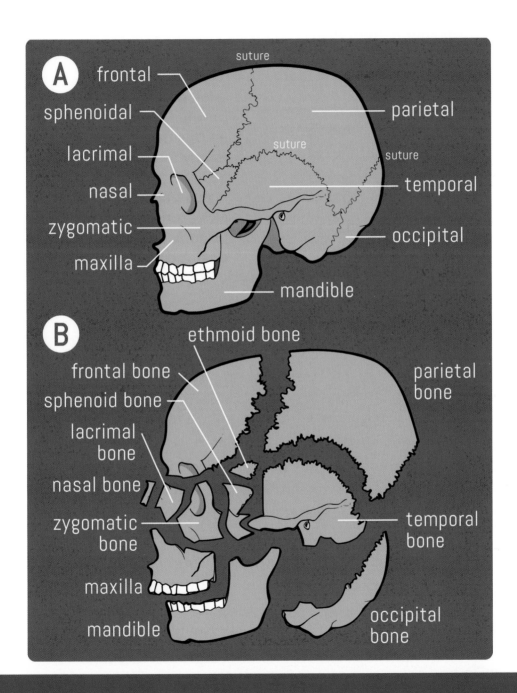

Figure 6. The human skull showing a) a side view and b) the individual bones that make up the skull. Sutures show where the bones have fused.

about one-third their adult size. The spaces between the skull bones allow the brain and head to grow. During its first year of life, a baby's brain weight increases from 400 g (14 oz) to 990 g (35 oz). By age six or seven, the brain is fully grown and weighs approximately 1,300 g (46 oz).

THINGS YOU WILL NEED

- **a friend, sibling, or parent (preferably one who is thin so you can easily feel his or her bones)**
- **if possible, a human skeleton or model (your school may have one you can borrow)**

This explains why a first grader's head appears to be too large for his or her body.

1. There are three bones in your middle ear (hammer, anvil, and stirrup) that move when sound waves cause your eardrum to vibrate. The only other bone in your head that moves is your mandible or lower jaw. It moves when you talk or chew. Your lower teeth are embedded in your mandible. The front part of your mandible is your chin, which you can easily locate and feel.

2. Beginning at your chin, feel back along one side of your mandible. The rear end of the mandible turns upward at almost 90 degrees. The end of

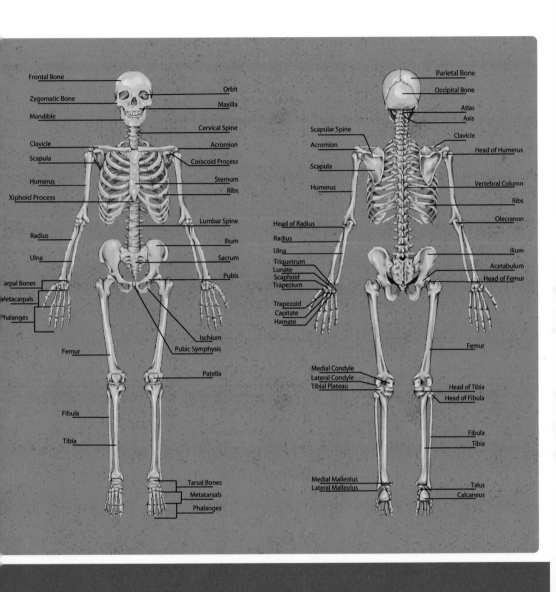

Figure 7. a) A diagram details the frontal view of a human skeleton. b) This human skeleton is seen from the back.

the mandible articulates (forms a joint) with the rest of the skull. It is connected to other fused bones of the head by ligaments. Tendons connect facial muscles to the mandible. The other end of the muscles are connected by tendons to skull bones that do not move. Contraction of these muscles move the mandible. This makes it possible for us to chew our food and to talk.

3. At the base of your neck, on either side, you can feel the clavicle (collar bone). Feeling along the clavicle, you'll find that it extends laterally (sideways) on both sides. Near the center of your upper chest it connects with your sternum (see Figure 7a). You can feel the outside of the sternum or breast bone. It extends down the center of your chest toward your abdomen. It narrows at its lower end to form a slightly pointed structure known as the xiphoid process.

4. The outer ends of your clavicle are connected to the scapulas (shoulder blades). Feel a partner's scapula. It has a ridge that ends at the acromion process (Figure 7b). It is the part of the scapula (shoulder blade) farthest from the middle of the body. Below the acromion process is a concave depression called the glenoid cavity (not shown).

5. The rounded end of the humerus (upper arm bone) fits into and can rotate in the glenoid cavity. You can feel the shaft of your humerus at the

center of your upper arm. But the upper end lies under the acromion process and muscle tissue. The lower end of the humerus is wide and articulates with the two bones of the lower arm.

6. What we normally call the elbow is the upper end of a lower arm bone, the ulna. If you follow the ulna downward, you will find that it ends in the knob-like styloid process above the little-finger side of the wrist.

7. The styloid process at the lower end of the other bone of the lower arm—the radius—can be found above the thumb-side of the wrist. Using your fingers, follow the radius upward to the point where it articulates with the humerus.

8. The wrist is made up of eight small bones called the carpals. They are difficult to identify individually. You can feel the five metacarpal bones on the back of your hand. The lower ends of these bones articulate with the phalanges, or fingers. There are a total of fourteen phalanges on each hand. Three are found in each finger and two in the thumb. The joints where metacarpals and phalanges meet are commonly known as your knuckles.

9. As you can see from Figure 8, many mammals have the same "arm" bones even though their relative sizes are very different. Such structures are said to be homologous because the bones have

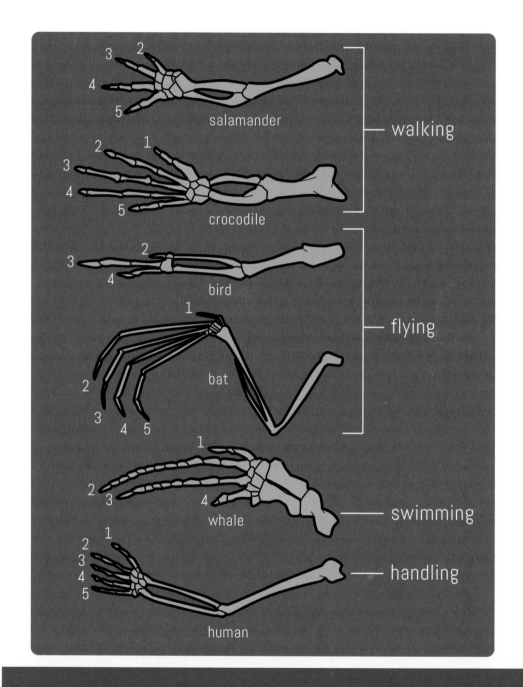

Figure 8. These forelimbs are homologous. What differences do you see? What similarities? What do the numbers indicate?

the same embryonic origin and basic structure even though they serve different purposes.

10. The skull sits atop the thirty-three bones that make up the vertebral column (see Figure 7). There are seven cervical vertebrae in the neck, twelve thoracic vertebrae at the rear of the chest, and five lumbar vertebrae in the lower back. The five sacral vertebrae and four coccygeal vertebrae fuse with one another and with the pelvis by adulthood. The fused sacral vertebrae are referred to as the sacrum. The fused coccygeal vertebrae are called the coccyx. In many animals the coccygeal vertebrae are separate and more numerous. They are the bones that lie within the animals' tails.

11. The vertebral column encloses and protects the spinal cord—the body's major nerve cells. These nerves connect the brain with the muscles and sensory cells of the body below the head. Many of the vertebrae have spinal processes (bony projections) that you can feel if you run your fingers along a friend's backbone. The thoracic vertebrae also have transverse processes that articulate with the twelve ribs on each side of the body, which you can also feel.

12. Feel the twelve ribs on each side of the vertebrae. They surround the lungs and heart, which lie within the upper body's thoracic cavity. Using your fingers, trace the path of one of the upper ribs. Start from a thoracic vertebrae on the back. Follow the rib, which

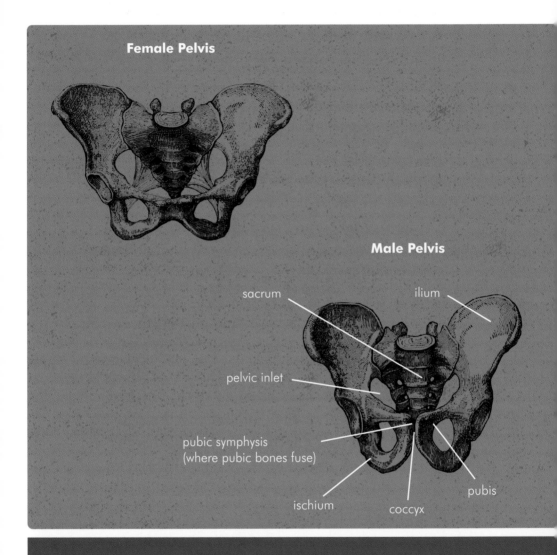

Female Pelvis

Male Pelvis

sacrum

ilium

pelvic inlet

pubic symphysis
(where pubic bones fuse)

ischium

coccyx

pubis

Figure 9. The female pelvis is wider and shallower than the male pelvis. Both have the same bones, though. They are simply slightly different in shape.

may pass under the scapula, to the sternum at the front of the body. The lower two ribs, which you can feel, are called "floating ribs." They do not attach to the sternum. The four pairs of ribs above the floating ribs join together. They form a common band of cartilage that attaches these ribs to the sternum above the xiphoid process. The remaining six pairs of ribs end in cartilage that connect them directly to the sternum. Some of these upper six pairs of ribs pass under the scapula so it is difficult to trace them all the way from vertebra to sternum.

13. The pelvis, shown in Figure 9, is similar in some ways to the shoulders. Just as the arms articulate with the shoulder bones, so the legs articulate with the pelvis. The rear of the pelvis is fused with the sacral and coccygeal vertebrae. It feels like a solid plate that covers the lower part of your back. The sides of the pelvis are formed by the ilium bones (hip bones) that you can feel on either side of your waist. The bottom of the pelvis consists of the ischium bones, the bones you sit on. The pubis bones form the front of the pelvis. They join to form the pubic symphysis at the middle of the very lowest part of your abdomen. You can feel them on either side of your body at the base of your groin.

14. The femur (upper leg bone) is the longest bone in your body. The rounded head at its upper end fits into a concavity in the pubis. You can feel the outer

upper end of the femur move as you walk. You can easily feel the very wide lower end of your femur. It lies behind your patella (knee cap).

15. The lower end of the femur articulates with the tibia (shin bone), the larger of the two bones of the lower leg. You can feel the entire front side of the tibia. Start just below the patella and follow it to its bulblike end on the inner (medial) side of your leg beside the ankle. The bulblike end of the tibia, the medial malleolus, has its mate on the other side of the ankle—the lateral malleolus. However, the lateral malleolus is the lower end of the fibula, which lies on the outer (lateral) side of your leg. How far can you trace a fibula up a leg?

Like the wrist, the ankle consists of a number of bones (seven)—the tarsals. The largest tarsal bone is the heel bone or calcaneus, which you can feel on the lower rear portion of your foot.

The metatarsals lie between the toes and the ankle and correspond to the metacarpal bones in the hand. You can probably feel all five of your metatarsals by moving your fingers over the top of your foot behind your toes.

The front ends of the metatarsals articulate with the phalanges, commonly known as toes. Your toes, like your fingers, have a total of fourteen phalanges on each foot. There are three phalanges in each of the four smaller toes and two in the great (big) toe.

You have now examined as many of the bones from your head to your toes that you could feel. Which bones were you not able to feel?

EXPLORING ON YOUR OWN

- On a real or plastic model of a human skeleton, or on detailed anatomical diagrams, identify all of the bones found in a human adult.
- Police often ask anthropologists to examine skeletal remains at crime scenes. Why do police ask anthropologists to examine skeletons? How do anthropologists distinguish between male and female skeletons? (See Figure 9.)
- Visit a science museum where the skeletons of different animals are on display. Can you identify bones similar to those found in humans in the bodies of these other animals?
- Broken bones—fractures—are a common injury. What are the various types of fractures and how are they treated?

THE ANATOMY OF JOINTS, WHERE BONES MEET

If you ever heard the old song about the head bone being connected to the neck bone and so on and so on, the joints are the places where those bones meet. Joints, however, come in many different forms. Some joints are fixed and do not allow movement. Other joints bend like hinges or move more freely like a ball and socket.

EXPERIMENT 9

JOINTS, AT THE JUNCTURE OF BONES

Let's examine some of the body's joints.

While you learn about all these joints, you can work with a partner to see if you can feel how they move.

FIXED JOINTS

1. Some of your joints are fixed. They do not allow movement. The bones of your skull, which were separate and distinct at birth, become fused as you age. The lines along which they join are known as sutures. Fixed joints are also found in many bones of your face.

SLIGHTLY MOVABLE JOINTS

2. Some bones meet at joints that allow limited movement. The ends of bones that meet in these joints are padded with cartilage and connected by slightly flexible ligaments. The lower ends of the tibia and fibula are joined by such ligaments so that these two bones may move slightly with respect to one another.

3. The cartilage between pelvic bones allows slight movement.

4. Between the vertebrae that make up your backbone, there are disks of cartilage that permit some twisting, compression, and extension. The movement of adjacent

vertebrae is limited. However, there are many vertebrae. As a result, your back has considerable flexibility. Through approximately what angle can you bend your back forward? Backward?

5. To see that many vertebrae make flexibility possible even though movement between any two vertebrae is limited, you can make a model of the vertebral column.

Take two soda straws. Cut one straw into ten or twelve pieces. Leave the other straw whole.

6. Next, run a length of string through each straw—the whole one and the one you cut into pieces.

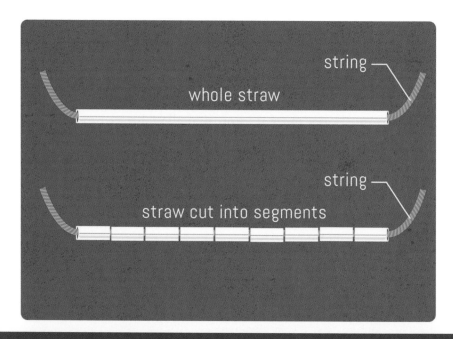

Figure 10. A straw cut into many segments can serve as a model of the vertebrae that make up a backbone. The cut-up straw and the uncut one are both suspended on strings. How do the two compare with regard to flexibility? Through what angle can you bend your back forward? Backward?

7. Hold the ends of each straw as shown in Figure 10. Which straw provides greater flexibility?

8. To see why it is advantageous to have many vertebrae, cut a third straw into three pieces and run a string through it. How does its flexibility compare with the straw that has ten or twelve segments?

MOVABLE JOINTS

Many joints are movable, but some allow greater movement than others. The ends of bones in movable joints are covered by cartilage. A membrane surrounds a fluid (synovial fluid) that lies between them. The fluid keeps the joint lubricated.

Pivot Joints

9. A pivot joint allows one bone to turn on another in much the same way that a faucet turns.
Turn your head from side to side and back and forth. You can do this because of a pivot joint. The first two cervical vertebrae—the atlas (the first or C-1 vertebra) and the axis (the second or C-2 vertebra)—form this pivot joint. The long vertical process of the axis, known as dens, fits into an opening in the anterior (front) side of the atlas. This allows the atlas, which is firmly attached to muscles of the head, to turn (pivot) on the axis.

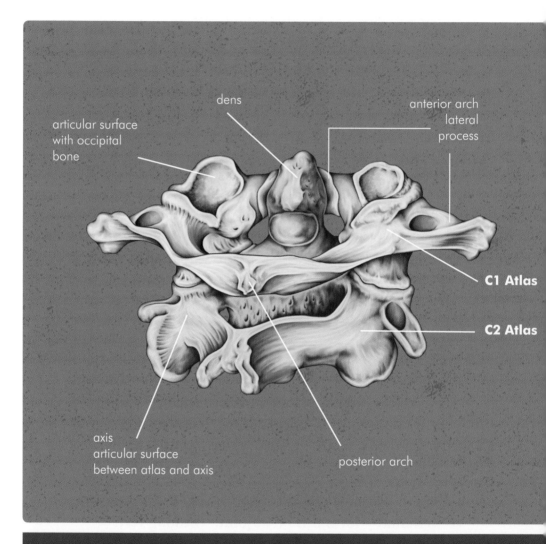

dens

articular surface
with occipital
bone

anterior arch
lateral
process

C1 Atlas

C2 Atlas

axis
articular surface
between atlas and axis

posterior arch

Figure 11. Rotation of the atlas on the axis, or C-1 on C-2, allows you to turn your head from side to side and back and forth.

As Figure 11 shows, the skull's occipital bone (shown in Figure 6) rests on the atlas's articular surfaces. When contracting neck muscles cause the atlas to turn on the axis, the head turns because its occipital bone articulates with the atlas.

Hinge Joints

10. Hinge joints allow bones to move in the same way that a door turns on its hinges. A door's hinge allows it to swing nearly 180 degrees, but no farther. Straighten your arm. Then bend it slowly.

    Which bones move? The joint between your humerus and your ulna and radius is a hinge joint. Is the joint between your femur and tibia at your knee a hinge joint? Are there other hinge joints in your body?

Ball-and-Socket Joints

11. When the sphere-shaped end of one bone fits into a cup like cavity in another bone, you may have a ball-and-socket joint. Such a joint allows movement in many directions, including rotation. At your shoulder, the end of the humerus fits into the scapula's glenoid cavity. The result is a very mobile ball-and-socket joint. Just ask any baseball pitcher. In how many different directions can you move your upper arm? Can it rotate in a complete circle?

    Your other ball-and-socket joint is where your hip and leg meet, at the articulation of your femur and pelvis. In how many directions can you move your upper leg? Why is it not as mobile as your shoulder joint?

Condyloid Joints

A condyloid joint is one in which the oval-shaped end (condyle) of one bone fits into the elliptical shaped cavity of another. The radius and one of the carpal bones behind your thumb form a condyloid joint at your wrist. What kind of motion does this type of joint allow?

Saddle Joints

In a saddle joint, the two bones that articulate both have convex and concave surfaces that mesh. The only saddle joints in your body are the joints formed by the metacarpal bones behind your thumbs and the carpal bones in your wrist.

Gliding Joints

A gliding joint, as its name implies, allows bones to glide over one another. Bones that meet in a gliding joint have nearly flat surfaces. Such joints are found between carpal and tarsal bones and between vertebrae. Can you detect the motion of any gliding joints with your fingers?

EXPLORING ON YOUR OWN

- A person's weight while standing can squeeze joints together, particularly the vertebrae. Could such squeezing change a person's height during the course of a day? Design and carry out an experiment to find out.

- Often, when you bend your knees, raise your arm, or "crack" your knuckles, you may hear a snapping sound. What causes such a sound?
- People who can contort their limbs and phalanges well beyond the normal range of flexibility are often said to be double-jointed. Are they really double-jointed?
- What is the origin of the terms *atlas* and *axis* for the first two cervical vertebrae?

EXPERIMENT 10

MAKING A JOINTLESS BODY

Doing this simple experiment will help you understand why joints are such an important part of a human's anatomy.

THINGS YOU WILL NEED

- **no materials are needed**

1. Stand in the center of a room.
2. Pretend all your joints are frozen. You can't bend your knees, arms, ankles, wrists, or even your fingers.

    Can you eat? Can you walk? Talk? Write? Turn your head? What can you do?

CHAPTER FOUR

THE ANATOMY OF HUMAN MUSCLES

Movements of your body, internal and external, visible and invisible, are caused by muscles. You're familiar with muscles that allow you to walk, run, and jump. However, you are probably not aware of muscles that cause motions inside your body. You've listened to one such muscle, your heart! Your cardiac, or heart, muscle contracts about once every second. That's a lot of heart beats over your lifetime. Imagine if you tried flexing your bicep muscle once a second all day long. You'd be very sore the next day!

You breathe because muscles move your ribs and diaphragm up and down without you having to think about the process. But there are muscles that are even more invisible to your daily existence. Muscles move food and fluids along your stomach and intestines. Muscles cause blood to move along the inside of your blood vessels. Clearly, muscles are a vital part of our anatomy. They account for nearly half your body mass.

All muscle tissue has the capacity to contract in response to an electrical stimulus from a nerve. When a muscle contracts, its length decreases. The contraction might cause a bone to move, reduce the diameter of a blood vessel, move food into your stomach, or push body waste along a section of your large intestine. But muscle can also stretch (extend) when a force pulls on it. And muscles, like rubber bands, are elastic. They will resume their original size after being stretched.

A muscle, like your biceps, consists of many elongated cells (muscle fibers) held together by connective tissue. But not all muscle is the same. There are three types of muscles. Striated muscle is so called because when seen under a microscope its cells have stripes. It is the type of muscle that makes bones move. It is also called voluntary muscle because you can voluntarily make it contract or relax. The biceps muscle on your upper arm is a striated or voluntary muscle. You can decide voluntarily to contract that muscle and lift your forearm.

Nonstriated or smooth muscles are also known as involuntary muscles. We cannot control them, nor are we normally aware of their action. You may, however, hear the results of their contraction. The gurgling sounds in your abdomen are due to the smooth muscle contractions of your stomach and intestines that cause fluids to move along your digestive tract.

The third type of muscle is cardiac muscle. It is found only in the heart. Its fibers have striations, but they are less distinct than in skeletal muscle and the cells are smaller.

The heart is really one large muscle. When its ventricles contract, they squeeze blood out of the heart into two major arteries—the aorta and the pulmonary artery. The pulmonary artery carries blood to the lungs; the aorta and its branches lead to all parts of the body.

When a muscle contracts, many fibers are stimulated. The total force exerted by the muscle depends on the number of fibers contracting. When you use a muscle to produce the maximum force it can provide, nearly all the fibers in the muscle contract. In most muscle activity, only a fraction of the fibers contract at any one time. Some fibers will contract while others relax. This helps to reduce muscle fatigue.

EXPERIMENT 11

INVOLUNTARY MUSCLES: CAN YOU SWALLOW WHILE UPSIDE DOWN?

Involuntary muscles surround your esophagus, stomach, and intestines, as well as your blood vessels. These are smooth muscles. They contract, but you are generally unaware of their action other than occasional gurgling sounds from your abdomen.

THINGS YOU WILL NEED

- **glass of water**
- **drinking straw**
- **an adult**

The movement of these muscles along the digestive tract is known as peristalsis. It is peristaltic action that moves food and waste matter along your digestive tract.

Normally, when you swallow food or liquids you are sitting at a table. You might assume that the force of gravity causes the food you swallow to move down your esophagus to your stomach and often gravity plays a role.

But wait! Let's think about this. We know that astronauts aboard the space station live for months in a condition of weightlessness. They must be able to swallow food. Perhaps there are smooth muscles along the esophagus that move food by peristalsis. Let's do an experiment to find out.

1. Place a glass of water with a drinking straw on the floor.
2. Ask an adult to support your feet so you can try to defy gravity by drinking water while upside down. (See Figure 12.)

Figure 12. Can you drink water while upside down?

3. Can you drink the water while your stomach and esophagus are above your mouth?
4. What can you conclude from this experiment?

EXPERIMENT 12

SOUNDS FROM A SWALLOW

From the previous experiment, you know that you can swallow while upside down. Gravity is not needed for food to travel down the esophagus to your stomach. It must be peristalsis that moves food and liquids along your digestive tract starting at the upper end of the esophagus.

THINGS YOU WILL NEED

- **stethoscope**
- **a partner**
- **glass of water**
- **stopwatch or watch with a second hand**
- **ruler**

You might wonder, "How long does it take for a peristaltic wave of smooth muscle to carry food from your mouth to your stomach?"

Let's do an experiment to find out.

1. Connect a stethoscope to your ears.
2. Place the chest piece of the stethoscope on a friend's abdomen about an inch below the xiphoid process (see Figure 7a).
3. Have your partner swallow some water. At the moment your partner swallows the water, have him or her start a stopwatch.

4. You will hear the water splash against the closed cardiac sphincter that separates the esophagus from the stomach. A short time later, when the peristaltic wave reaches the sphincter (valve), you will hear the water pass through the open sphincter into the stomach. When you hear that second sound, say, "Stop!"

5. Your partner will stop the watch or note the exact time on a watch with a second hand or mode.

   How long did it take for the peristaltic wave to pass along the length of the esophagus? How can you use that time and another measurement to estimate the speed at which the peristaltic wave traveled along the esophagus?

EXPERIMENT **13**

SOME OF YOUR BODY'S VOLUNTARY MUSCLES

You have hundreds of skeletal muscles in your body. As a result, you can move your body and its parts in many different ways. A

> **THINGS YOU WILL NEED**
>
> • **no materials are needed**

skeletal muscle has an origin and an insertion. Its origin (the attachment of one end) is on a bone that remains relatively fixed. Its other end, its insertion, is attached to a bone that moves when the muscle contracts. Both attachments are made with fibrous tendons. Remember, tendons connect muscles to bones.

In this experiment, you will feel and identify some of the muscles shown in Figure 13. This figure will be useful in helping you locate particular muscles.

One of your largest muscles is your quadriceps femoris (thigh muscle). It has a tendon that goes around the patella (knee cap) and inserts on the tibia. It is the tendon you tapped to obtain the patellar reflex in Experiment 5.

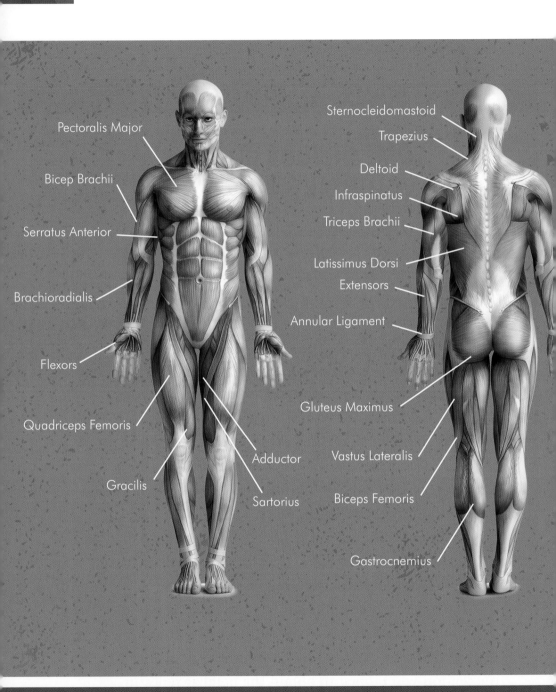

Figure 13. The major muscles of the body are seen from the back, side, and front.

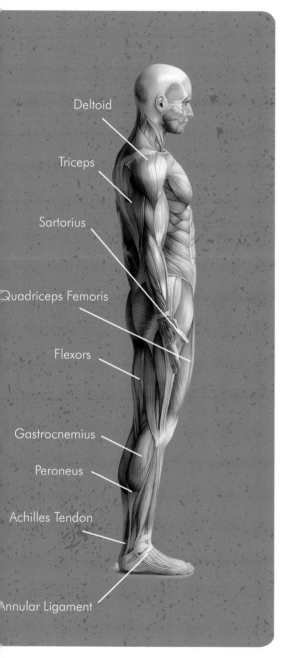

Deltoid

Triceps

Sartorius

Quadriceps Femoris

Flexors

Gastrocnemius

Peroneus

Achilles Tendon

Annular Ligament

1. Put the fingers of one hand on that tendon just below your patella.
2. Put the fingers of your other hand on your quadriceps femoris a few inches above your patella.
3. Slowly contract your quadriceps. At the same time feel its tendon just below the patella. Notice how the tendon tightens as the quadriceps contracts.
4. Continue to contract your quadriceps. Notice how, through the tendon, it raises your lower leg.

Another muscle you may recognize is the biceps muscle on your upper arm. To a doctor it is your biceps brachii. The *bi-* part of the word *biceps* means the muscle has two parts and two origins. The *brachii* part is from the Latin word *brachium*, which means "arm."

Both origins of biceps bronchii are on the shoulder. Its insertion is at the upper end of the radius bone of the lower arm.

5. Place your left arm at your side.

6. Put your right hand on your left biceps. Then contract your left biceps. As the muscle contracts and shortens, two things happen. The radius bone is lifted (and with it the lower arm). At the same time, the radius is turned outward so that the palm of your hand turns upward.

7. Put the fingers of your right hand on the inside of your elbow near the base of your left biceps. As you slowly contract the biceps, feel the tension in the tendon that inserts on the radius raising the lower arm.

8. You can use another muscle—the brachialis— to bend your arm. The brachialis lies under the biceps. Its origin is on the humerus bone. Its insertion is on the ulna.

9. Bend your arm again, but this time keep your palm turned downward so that the radius does not turn about the ulna. As you can feel, the biceps does not contract. Rather, it gets raised a little by the contracting brachialis muscle. The upper arm feels more flaccid than it did before.

10. Now, turn the palm up. You can feel the biceps pop up.

    If a bone can be moved, it can be returned to where it was before being moved. Muscles are paired so that movements can be reversed. You can flex (bend) your arm by contracting your biceps or brachialis muscles. There is also is a muscle that can extend (straighten) the arm. The muscle that straightens your arm is the triceps brachii. What does its name tell you?

11. Flex your right arm. Next, put your left hand on the back of your right upper arm. Feel the triceps contract as you straighten your arm. What can you assume about the location of the triceps' insertion? Feel the tendon leading to that insertion at the lower end of the triceps. Was your assumption correct?

12. The muscle that extends your fingers is the extensor digitorum communis (Figure 14). Feel that muscle on the upper side of your lower arm when you extend your fingers. As the fingers extend, notice that beneath the skin on the back of your hand you can see the movement of the tendons that connect the muscle to the fingers. Extending your index finger alone will enable you to see a single tendon moving beneath the skin. Can each finger and thumb be extended alone?

13. Figure 14 shows the flexor digitorum profundus, which you use to bend your fingers. Place your

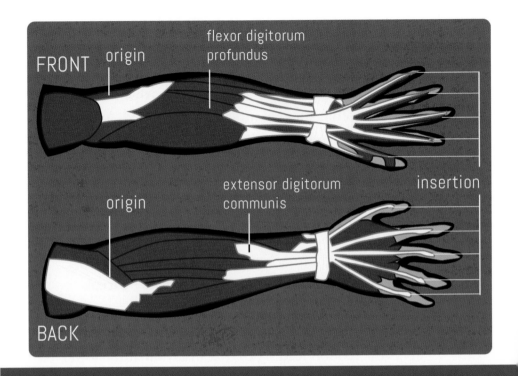

Figure 14. Opposing muscles a) extend and b) flex the fingers of the hand.

fingers on the inside of your opposite forearm and feel this muscle contract. At the same time, watch the tendons that connect this muscle to the fingers move beneath the skin on your forearm. Can you find the muscles that extend and flex your thumbs? Can you see the movement of the tendons that connect these muscles to the thumbs?

EXPLORING ON YOUR OWN

- What is the advantage of having the muscles that control the fingers and thumbs located so far from the hands?
- The gastrocnemius and soleus muscles in your calf are connected to your heel bone by the Achilles tendon. It is the strongest and thickest tendon in your body. You will find the story of Achilles in a book on Greek mythology. After reading the story, explain why this tendon was named for him.

EXPERIMENT 14

SOME ADDITIONAL VOLUNTARY MUSCLES

Figure 15 shows some large muscles on the front of your upper body. Let's look for the origins and insertions of these muscles. Let's also see what happens when these muscles contract.

THINGS YOU WILL NEED

• **a partner**

1. Feel one of the deltoid muscles on the top of a shoulder.
2. Raise your arm or have a partner raise his or her arm. Feel along the deltoid muscle as it contracts. Feel the tendons connecting it to its origin along the clavicle.
3. Again, look for a tendon at the other end of the deltoid as it contracts lifting the arm. Can you feel its insertion on the humerus?
4. Feel a pectoralis major muscle as you or your partner flexes one of the pectorals. You'll find its origin on the sternum.

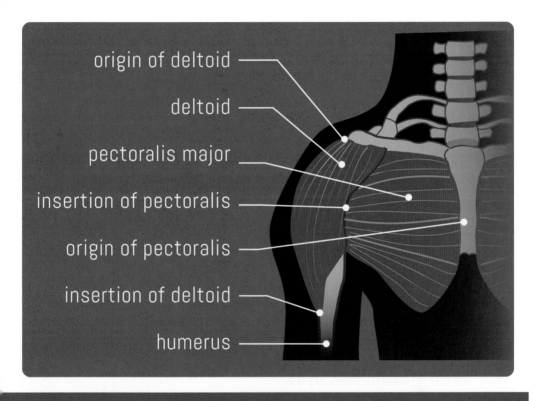

origin of deltoid

deltoid

pectoralis major

insertion of pectoralis

origin of pectoralis

insertion of deltoid

humerus

Figure 15. These muscles have opposing effects on the humerus. The deltoids (there is another on the back that has its origin on the scapula) lift the humerus. The pectoralis lowers the humerus.

The pectoralis muscle is used to lower a raised arm. As it contracts, pulling a raised arm downward, you can feel its tendon just in front of the arm pit. Search for its insertion on the humerus.

EXPERIMENT 15

MUSCLES COME IN PAIRS

Muscles contract; they do not expand. Consequently, muscle forces are pulls, not pushes. If a muscle bends a joint, another muscle must pull in the opposite way to straighten the joint.

You have seen some muscle pairs. The biceps bends the arm; the triceps straightens the arm. The deltoid raises the arm; the pectoralis lowers the arm. Muscle pairs are often not of equal strength. You can use a bathroom scale to compare the strengths of muscle pairs.

If you play soccer, you know there are muscles that enable you to kick both forward and backward. Do they have equal strength?

1. To find out, stand facing a wall. Place a bathroom scale upright against the wall (Figure 16a). With what force can you push your foot forward against the scale? You may need a partner to read the scale.

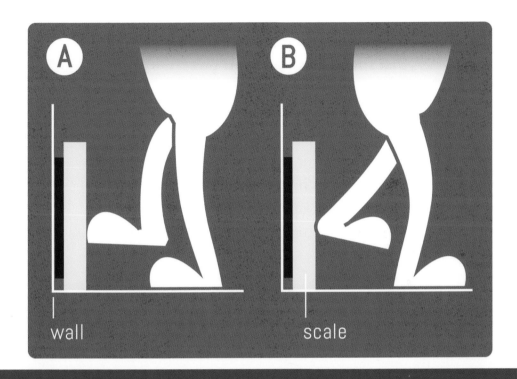

wall

scale

Figure 16. Which kicking muscle is stronger? Or are they of equal strength? a) Push your foot forward against the scale. With what force, in pounds, can you push forward? b) Push your foot backward against the scale. With what force can you push backward?

2. Now place your heel against the scale (Figure 16b). With what force can you push backward? Have a partner observe the scale.

      Are the muscle pairs equal in strength? If not, which member of the pair is stronger?

3. Figure out ways to compare the strengths of other muscle pairs.

      For example, how does the strength of the biceps and brachialis muscles that bend your arm compare with the strength of the triceps muscle that straightens your arm?

4. Compare the strengths of the muscles in the pairs used to:

   (1) turn your toes upward or downward;

   (2) squeeze your fingers into a fist or open them;

   (3) move your head forward or backward;

   (4) move your upper arm forward or backward;

   (5) bend or straighten your leg at the knee.

EXPERIMENT 16

MUSCLE FATIGUE

Muscles tire with use. No one can do physical work or exercise for an unlimited time period. We have to stop and rest.

THINGS YOU WILL NEED

- **bathroom scale**

1. Pick up the bathroom scale you used in the previous experiment. Hold it in your hands. Squeeze the scale as tightly as you can with just your hands. What is the maximum squeeze force you can exert on the scale with your hands?

2. Next, open and close your hands to make and open a fist as fast as you can for a minute or until you cannot do it anymore.

3. Now squeeze the scale again. How strong are your hands now? With what force can they squeeze the scale? How can you explain any difference in hand strength?

EXPLORING ON YOUR OWN

- As you have seen, fatigue affects the short-term strength of a muscle. Does it also affect your ability to control the muscle? Design an experiment to find out.

- Walking on two legs rather than four has disadvantages. It can result in lower back pain, torn knee cartilages, broken hips, varicose veins, hernias, and fallen arches. However, it does free our hands to perform the tasks that distinguish us from other animals. We can use our hands to carry food, to make and use tools, and to write—a means of communication unknown to other animals.

  Our hands have what are known as opposable thumbs, which give us another advantage over other animals. To see what that means, notice that you can touch the tips of any of your other fingers with your thumb. To see the value provided by an opposable thumb, have someone tape your thumbs to your palms so that you cannot use them. What tasks are now difficult or impossible to perform?

EXPERIMENT 17

ACTIVE MUSCLES

To avoid fatigue, your muscle fibers do not usually all contract at the same time. While some contract, others are inactive. As a result, your muscle fibers are constantly sharing the workload. Evidence of this can be found by doing a simple experiment.

THINGS YOU WILL NEED

- **paper clip**
- **butter knife**
- **table or counter top**

1. Partially open a paper clip.
2. Hang it on the end of a butter knife as shown in Figure 17.
3. Hold the tip of the paper clip as close as possible to a table or counter top without touching it. Do you occasionally hear the tip of the paper clip touching the table. Why do you think you are unable to hold the paper clip perfectly still?
4. Repeat this experiment after exercising. Open and close your hands to make a fist as fast as you can for a minute or until you cannot do it anymore. Then try to hold the paper clip perfectly still at the end

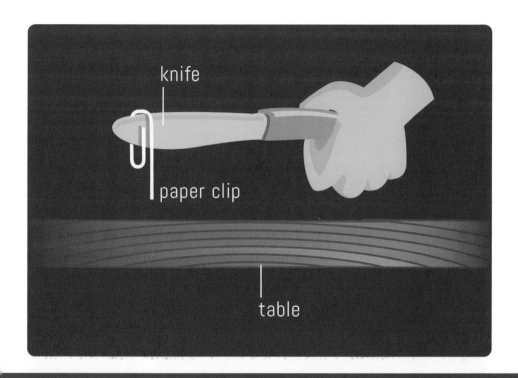

Figure 17. Can you hold a paper clip hanging from the end of a butter knife perfectly still? If not, why can't you?

of the knife. What effect does exercise have on your ability to control your muscles? How can you explain the effect?

MUSCLES AND LEVERS

In the human body, muscles and bones act together as levers. A simple lever is a rigid rod that is free to turn about a fixed point of support called the fulcrum. When in use, two forces act on

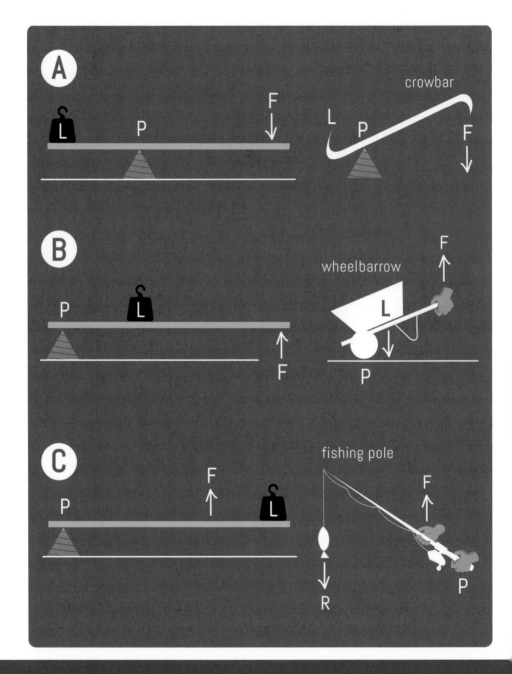

Figure 18. Levers: a) A first-class lever. b) A second-class lever. c) A third-class lever. P indicates the fulcrum; it is the point about which the lever turns. L indicates the load, and F indicates the force being applied.

the lever at different points. One force, the resistance force, may be regarded as something, such as a weight, to be lifted, moved, or balanced. The second force, the effort force, is used to overcome, lift, or balance the resistance force.

Levers can be divided into three classes. The class depends on the location of the resistance and effort forces relative to the fulcrum. The three classes of levers are shown in Figure 18. A first-class lever, such as a crowbar, has the resistance force L (for load) and the effort force F (for force) on opposite sides of the fulcrum (the point P), about which the lever turns.

With a second-class lever (Figure 18b), such as a wheelbarrow, the load and the force are both on the same side of the lever, but the effort force is farther from the fulcrum than the load or resistance.

In a third-class lever, such as a fishing pole, the load and effort force are again on the same side of the lever. But the resistance force or load is farther from the fulcrum than the effort force.

For any resistance force, such as a weight, we can predict the effort force needed to balance the resistance because of a scientific law based on experiments. This law tells us that for the resistance force, R, to be balanced by the effort force, e, e × D (the distance of the effort force from the fulcrum) must at least be equal to R × d (the distance of the resistance from the fulcrum).

An example of a balanced lever is shown in Figure 19. As you can see R × d = e × D, or, in this case, 100 kg × 0.25 m = 25 kg × 1.00 m.

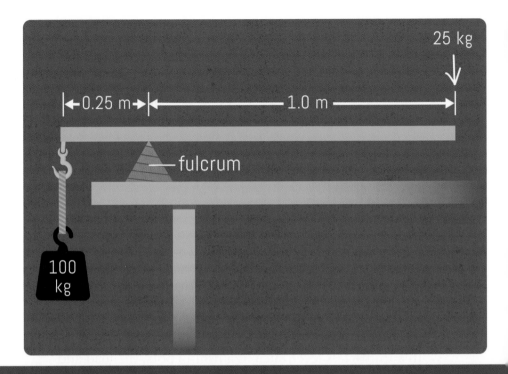

Figure 19. In this lever, a 100 kg weight at a distance of 0.25 m from the fulcrum is balanced by a force of 25 kg at a distance of 1.0 m from the fulcrum.

100 kg × 0.25 m = 25 kg × 1.0 m.

Mathematically this can be stated as R x d = e × D, where R is the resistance, d is its distance from the fulcrum, e is effort force, and D is its distance from the fulcrum. Of course, in practice e x D must be slightly greater than R × d if the effort force is to lift the resistance. Can you explain why?

EXPERIMENT 18

MUSCLES AND A BODY LEVER

There are many muscles and bones that act as levers in your body. One such lever is your forearm.

Hold a weight in your hand. Feel the tendons from the brachialis and biceps muscles as you bend your arm at the elbow and raise the weight. Figure 20 shows how this third-class lever works. How will the effort force, F, exerted by the muscle, compare with the resistance R—the weight being lifted?

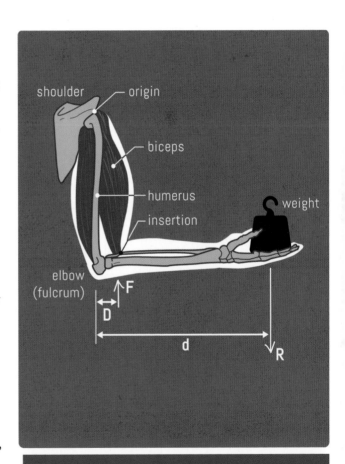

Figure 20. To lift a weight, the biceps contracts, lifting the forearm and the hand holding the weight. The elbow acts as a fulcrum. The biceps provides the effort force at its insertion on the radius. In this third-class lever, F × D must be slightly larger than R × d.

Based on your knowledge of third-class levers, do you think you could lift more with your fingers, your wrist, or your forearm?

1. To find out, place a bathroom scale against the underside of a heavy table or counter. Let the dial extend out far enough so that you can see it.
2. Sit in front of the scale with your forearm at a right angle and in contact with the scale. (Sit on pillows if necessary.)
3. Wrap a small block of wood in some soft cloth. With the block on your fingers or lower arm, push against the scale.
4. Using your fingertips, with how much force can you push upward?
5. Using your wrist, with how much force can you push upward?
6. Using your forearm, with how much force can you push upward?

   Explain your results based on your knowledge of levers. Do the results of this experiment agree with your predictions?
7. Estimate the effort force that your muscle must exert to create each force that you pushed on the scale.

EXPLORING ON YOUR OWN

- What other examples of muscles acting as levers can you find in your body? Are they all third-class levers?
- When you exercise, you use your muscles. What is the difference between (a) isotonic and isometric exercises and (b) aerobic and anaerobic exercise?

EXPERIMENT **19**

BALANCE AND YOUR CENTER OF MASS (COM)

Doctors are often concerned about a patient's balance, particularly with older patients. Poor balance can lead to falls, broken bones, even death. As a doctor, you might counsel patients to keep their center of mass at a point above and between their feet.

The patient will likely ask, "What is my center of mass?" You may be asking the same question right now.

Every object, and person, has a center of mass (COM)—a point where all its mass can be considered to be located. It is the balance point of an object or person, a point where there is no tendency to rotate one way or the other. It is the point where you can pick up the object without it turning clockwise or counterclockwise.

The COM of a sphere, such as Earth or a baseball, is its center. Where do you think the COM of a yardstick is located? What about your body? Let's find out!

1. Place a yardstick on your outstretched hand (Figure 21). Where can you place the yardstick so it balances and doesn't rotate and fall? Where do you think the yardstick's COM is located? Is the yardstick balanced and not rotating or falling? If it is, you have found its COM.

2. Not all objects are as uniform as a sphere or a yard-stick. Your own body is not uniform; yet, it must have a center of mass.

3. To find the approximate location of your COM, lie on the arm of a sofa. Keep your arms at your side and your lower abdomen on the sofa's arm. Your COM is likely a few centimeters below your belly button.

4. Adjust your position until your body is balanced on the arm of the sofa. When your body is balanced on the chair, your COM lies directly above the arm of the sofa. Of course, that point is inside your body about half way from your abdomen to your back.

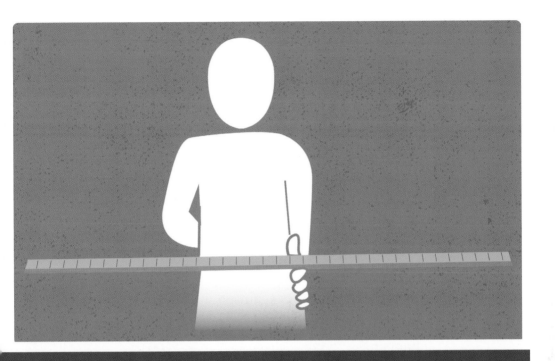

Figure 21. Where is the yardstick's center of mass? Where is your center of mass?

5. Normally, you keep your COM above and between your two feet. By so doing, there is no tendency for your body to rotate and fall.

6. How does your body respond when your COM is beyond points of support? To find out, stand with your right foot and right shoulder against a wall. Now, lift your left foot. What happens? How do you adjust?

7. Stand in front of a full-length mirror. Lift one foot so you have only one point of support. How does your body respond? What happens to your COM?

Here are some other human body COM experiments to try.

8. Stand sideways to the front of a full-length mirror. Watch what your body does as you bend to touch your toes. Where does your COM go as you lower your arms and shoulders toward your toes? Why must your COM move this way if you are to remain on your feet?

9. Look in the same mirror as you move from a normal flat-footed stance to one where you stand on your toes. How does your COM move? Why does it move that way?

10. Stand with your toes against a wall. Then try to stand on your toes. Try it! What happens? Why does it happen?

11. Here is a fun thing to try at a party or in science class. It can help locate a person's COM.

   Ask someone to get on the floor on his hands and knees. Place a pack of cards, a blackboard eraser, or an upright long thin wooden block one cubit in front of his knees. (A cubit is the distance from a person's elbow to the fingertips of his outstretched hand.)

   Now, the person, with hands behind his back, is to try to tip the cards, the eraser, or the block over with his nose. Do this with different people. Keep your eyes on participants' COM as they attempt to knock over the upright object. How is their COM related to their ability to maintain their balance?

How many people can do this? What does it have to do with a person's COM? Are women and girls more able to do this more than men and boys? Does COM seem to be gender related?

COM AND DOCTORS

As a doctor, having explained center of mass to a fall-prone patient, you might recommend he or she use a cane. A cane provides a third point within which a patient may confine his or her center of mass. For some patients, you might even recommend two canes. The patient would now, like a four-legged animal, have four points to support his center of mass. Crutches provide yet another way to give someone "four legs" to surround a person's COM. You don't see four-legged animals fall very often, even when running and it's not likely you'll see someone running with two canes or two crutches!

CHAPTER FIVE

BREATHING: THE EXCHANGE OF OXYGEN AND CARBON DIOXIDE

Respiration is the exchange of carbon dioxide for oxygen. The cells in our bodies need oxygen to carry on life processes. Carbon dioxide is the waste product that results when oxygen combines with food substances to provide the energy our cells need to do their work.

You may have heard someone say, "We inhale oxygen and exhale carbon dioxide."

That statement is false. It would be more correct to say we inhale air and we exhale air. The air we inhale and the air we exhale do differ, but not by much. The following table gives the average concentration of gases found in inhaled and exhaled air.

As you can see, the concentration of oxygen in exhaled air decreases by about 3 to 5 percent and the concentration of carbon dioxide increases by about 4 to 5 percent. The exchange of gases is nowhere near perfect. The short time that inhaled air remains in the lungs before being exhaled limits the amount of oxygen that can be absorbed by the blood. It also limits the amount of carbon dioxide that can be released from the blood to the air.

Table: Concentration of gases, by volume, in inhaled and exhaled air.

Gas	Concentration in Inhaled Air	Concentration in Exhaled Air
Nitrogen (N_2)	78	78
Oxygen (O_2)	21	16–18.6
Argon (Ar)	1	1
Carbon dioxide (CO_2)	0.04	4–5.3

The exchange of gases takes place in the tiny alveoli (air sacs) at the ends of the small bronchial tubes that carry air from and to the mouth and nose. Capillaries surround the alveoli. And it is through the walls of these capillaries and alveoli that gases diffuse from blood to air and air to blood.

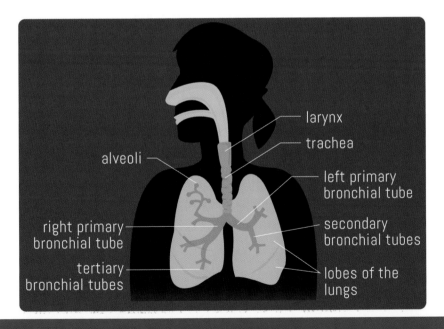

Figure 22. Air passes from the mouth or nose to the trachea, bronchial tubes, and eventually to the alveoli where gases (oxygen and carbon dioxide) are exchanged between blood and air.

EXPERIMENT 20

WHAT HAPPENS WHEN WE BREATHE?

Right now while you read these words your body is breathing, automatically without you having to think about the process. Nerve impulses from the brain stem cause us to breathe.

That nerve center is influenced by the concentration of carbon dioxide in the blood. As you probably suspect, an increase in carbon dioxide will stimulate an increase in breathing rate because more oxygen is needed.

1. Wrap a cloth measuring tape around a partner's chest. What happens to the circumference of your partner's chest when he or she takes a deep breath?
2. Ask your partner to exhale as much air as possible. What happens to the circumference of his or her chest?
3. Wrap the tape measure around your partner's abdomen at about the level of his or her navel (belly button). What happens to the circumference of the abdomen when your partner takes a deep breath? What happens to it after he or she exhales as much air as possible?

WHAT'S HAPPENING?

As you have seen, your partner's abdomen and chest both grew in circumference when he or she inhaled. These changes were caused by the contraction of his diaphragm. The diaphragm (see Figure 23) is a large muscle that separates the chest and abdominal cavities. The chest, or thoracic cavity, contains your

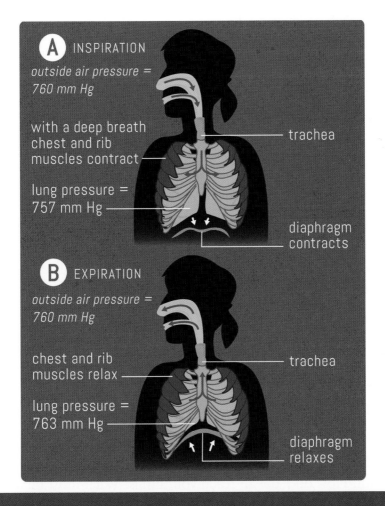

(A) INSPIRATION

outside air pressure = 760 mm Hg

with a deep breath chest and rib muscles contract

lung pressure = 757 mm Hg

trachea

diaphragm contracts

(B) EXPIRATION

outside air pressure = 760 mm Hg

chest and rib muscles relax

lung pressure = 763 mm Hg

trachea

diaphragm relaxes

Figure 23. The diaphragm is the main breathing muscle. These drawings show how it moves and causes us to inhale and exhale.

heart and lungs; the abdominal cavity holds your stomach, liver, kidneys and intestines, as well as other smaller organs.

When your diaphragm contracts, it pushes your stomach and the other organs in your abdomen downward. This causes your abdomen to increase in circumference because the same volume of organs are squeezed into a smaller space. At the same time, the size of your thoracic cavity increases as the contracting diaphragm moves downward while intercostal muscles in your chest lift your ribs upward and outward. The increased volume of the chest cavity reduces the air pressure in your lungs. The air pressure outside your body becomes greater than the pressure inside your lungs. As a result, air flows into your lungs as you inhale. The inhaled air travels along the trachea and bronchial tubes. The bronchial tubes branch into smaller and smaller tubes that finally end in tiny air sacs called alveoli. Alveoli are surrounded by capillaries. The concentration of oxygen in the blood is less than in the air in the alveoli. Consequently, oxygen diffuses from air to blood. At the same time, carbon dioxide passes from blood to air in the alveoli.

When you exhale, the rib cage falls, the diaphragm muscle relaxes and rises, the chest cavity becomes smaller. As this happens, the air pressure in your lungs increases until it exceeds the air pressure outside. Air is then forced out of your lungs through your nostrils or mouth—you exhale.

When you have a cold and your nose is filled with mucus, you can still breathe. To see why, hold your nose. Can you still breathe? How does air reach your lungs? Now close your mouth. How does the air reach your lungs? What must be true about your mouth and nose? Refer to Figure 22.

EXPLORING ON YOUR OWN

What causes hiccups? How are they related to breathing? There are lots of "cures" for hiccups. Do any of them work?

EXPERIMENT 21

A MODEL OF A LUNG

You can make a model that will show you how a lung works.

THINGS YOU WILL NEED

- **sharp knife or shears**
- **clear plastic soda bottle**
- **large strong rubber band**
- **good-size rubber balloon that has been blown up several times**
- **clear plastic wrap**
- **scissors**
- **partner**

1. **Ask an adult** to cut off the bottom of a clear, plastic soda bottle.
2. Insert a good-sized balloon into the bottle. The balloon will be a model of a lung. Pull the neck of the balloon over the mouth of the bottle so that air can enter and leave the balloon. See Figure 24.

3. To represent the diaphragm, stretch a sheet of clear plastic wrap over the open bottom of the bottle.

4. To keep the plastic wrap in its stretched position, place one or more strong rubber bands around the plastic near the cutoff bottom of the bottle as shown in the drawing. You may need a partner to help you.

5. Attach half a strip of clear plastic tape to the center of the plastic wrap as shown. Leave the other half free so you can use it to pull on the "diaphragm."

6. What happens to the balloon (lung) inside the bottle (chest cavity) when you pull down on the "diaphragm?" Why does it happen?

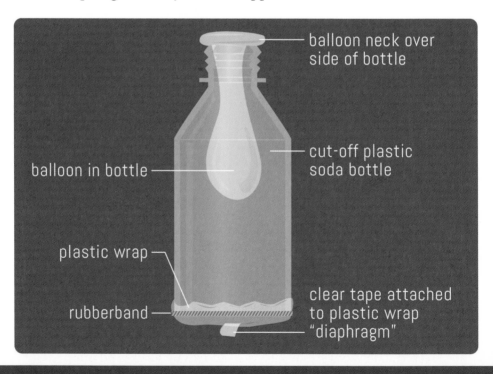

Figure 24. A model of a lung shows how air is inhaled and exhaled.

7. What happens to the balloon when the diaphragm returns to its original position? Why does it happen?

    In a real lung, there is a thin sac between the lung and the chest wall that keeps the lung attached to the chest wall. As a result, the lung, unlike the balloon, doesn't collapse when air is exhaled.

EXPERIMENT 22

HOW MUCH AIR DO YOU BREATHE?

When you tested the lungs (Experiment 3), you heard air move into the lungs. This movement of air takes place a number of times each minute.

Doctors measure the volume of air that you breathe with a device known as a spirometer. But you can make reasonably accurate measurements of the volume with a plastic bag and a pail of water.

The volume of air you normally inhale and exhale is called your tidal air. The additional air that you can inhale after taking in a normal breath is called your complemental air. It is the extra air you inhale when you take a deep breath. The volume of air you can exhale after a normal expiration of tidal air is called your supplemental air. Even after forcing out your supplemental air, about 1.2 liters (1.3 quarts) of air remains. This is your residual air.

THINGS YOU WILL NEED

- **a partner**
- **2 large, rigid, transparent or semitransparent plastic containers, one with a volume of about 3–4 L (1 gal)**
- **a second container about twice as large**
- **tape**
- **marking pen**
- **large graduated cylinder or measuring cup**
- **1-L or 1-qt plastic bag**
- **twist tie**
- **clock or watch**
- **calculator (optional)**
- **pen or pencil**
- **notebook**
- **2-L or 2-qt plastic bag**
- **5-L or 2-gal plastic bag**
- **people of different age, gender, height, weight, and chest size**

1. To measure your tidal air, first calibrate a large, rigid, transparent or semitransparent plastic container. Place a strip of narrow tape vertically along the side of the container. Then pour known volumes, say increments of 100 mL of water, into the container and mark the water levels of the different volumes with a marking pen.

2. Pour some water into the container until the water level is on one of the lines you marked.

3. Hold your nose so that the air you breathe goes through your mouth.

4. When you have adjusted to mouth breathing, place the opening of a 1-L or 1-qt plastic bag (from which all the air has been removed) firmly around your mouth just before you exhale. Collect the exhaled air in the bag. (Do not blow, just exhale in a normal way.)

5. Twist the neck of the bag to seal off the exhaled air. Seal the bag with a twist tie. **Caution: Never pull a plastic bag over your head.**

6. Holding the bag of air in your hand, push it under the water in the calibrated container as shown in Figure 25a. Mark the water level in the container before and after submerging the bag. Also mark your wrist at the water level.

7. Finally, squeeze all the air out of the bag, hold it in your fist, and put your fist back into the water up to the mark on your

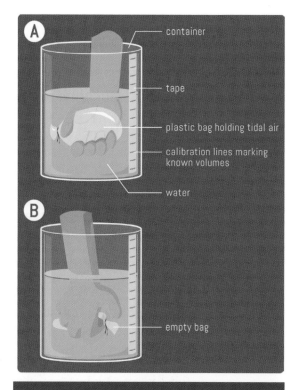

Figure 25. This experiment will allow you to measure the volume of the tidal air you breathe.

wrist (Figure 25b). What is the volume of your hand and the empty bag? How can you find the volume of your tidal air?

8. Determine your breathing rate by counting the number of times you breathe in one minute. Repeat this several times and take an average. From all your data, what volume of air do you breathe in one hour? In one day?

9. After exhaling your normal tidal air (a normal exhale), place a two-liter or two-quart plastic bag firmly around your mouth. Exhale as much additional air as possible into the bag. Seal the bag and immerse it in water as before. What is the volume of your supplemental air?

10. To measure your vital capacity, you will need a calibrated container that is about twice as large as the one you have been using. Calibrate the large container.

11. Inhale the deepest breath you can. Then exhale as much air as you can into a 5-L or 2-gal plastic bag and seal the bag. Use the large calibrated container to find the volume of the air you exhaled.

     The large volume of air you exhaled is called your vital capacity. Show that it is approximately the sum of your complemental, tidal, and supplemental airs. What is your vital capacity?

12. From all your measurements, what is the maximum volume of air that your lungs can hold? (Don't forget the 1.2 liters of residual air.)

13. Compare the vital capacities of a number of people. Are these volumes related to age? To gender? To height or weight? To chest size?

EXPLORING ON YOUR OWN

- How did scientists determine the volume of residual air?
- Is breathing rate related to age or gender? (Be sure to measure a baby's breathing rate.) Is it related to activity? How do sleep and exercise affect breathing rate?

EXPERIMENT **23**

AIR, LUNG AIR, AND CARBON DIOXIDE

Because matches are involved in this experiment, it should be done under adult supervision.

As you know, the air you inhale is richer in oxygen than the air you exhale. And the air you exhale is richer in carbon dioxide than the air you inhale.

This experiment provides one way to see, qualitatively, if exhaled air really has more carbon dioxide than ordinary air.

It is done by comparing the time that a candle will burn in a volume of air with the time it will burn in the same volume of air exhaled from your lungs.

1. Use a small piece of clay to support a birthday candle (Figure 26a).
2. **Under adult supervision**, light the candle.
3. After the candle has burned for about twenty seconds, invert an empty one-quart jar. Put the inverted jar over the candle (Figure 26b). Use a clock or a watch that can measure seconds to record how long the candle burns in the air-filled jar. Why do you think it finally goes out?
4. To see how long the candle will burn in lung air, relight the candle **under adult supervision**.
5. Fill the jar with water, cover its mouth with a square piece of cardboard, and invert it (Figure 26c).
6. Lower the jar into a pan of water. Then remove the cardboard square (Figure 26d). Air pressure will keep the water in the jar.
7. Next, take a deep breath. Immediately expel all the

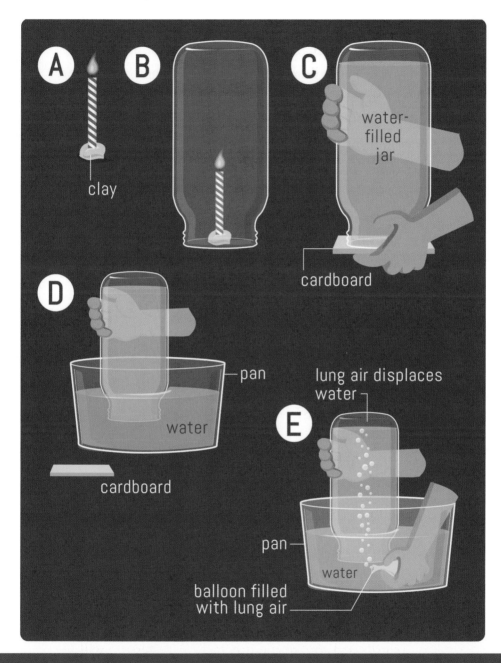

Figure 26. a) A birthday candle will burn in air for as long as the wax lasts. b) How long will a candle burn in a liter or quart-jar of air? c) Fill the jar with water, cover the jar's mouth and invert the jar. d) Lower the jar into a pan of water and remove the cover. e) Fill the jar with the lung air you collect in a balloon. How long will the candle burn in a quart or liter of lung air?

lung air in that breath to fill a balloon. Seal the neck of the balloon with your fingers.

8. Place the balloon's mouth under the mouth of the water-filled jar. Slowly let the lung air escape into the jar (Figure 26e). The lung air will replace the water in the jar.

9. Continue to put lung air into the jar until all the water is replaced. Once the jar is filled with lung air, remove it from the water and quickly place it over the burning candle. For how long does the candle burn in lung air? Record the time.

10. Repeat the experiment, but this time hold the air in your lungs for about twenty seconds before you use it to fill the balloon.

    How long do you think the candle will burn in lung air that has been in your lungs for twenty seconds? Make a prediction.

11. Then place the jar filled with lung air over the candle. Is the candle's burn time different than when you filled the balloon with lung air that had not been in your lungs as long? Was your prediction correct? If it was, can you explain why? If it wasn't, can you explain why it wasn't?

TESTING FOR CARBON DIOXIDE IN INHALED AND EXHALED AIR

Limewater is a solution of calcium hydroxide [$Ca(OH)_2$]. It reacts with carbon dioxide (CO_2) to form a milky white precipitate of calcium carbonate ($CaCO_3$). Chemists use limewater to test for the presence of carbon dioxide.

THINGS YOU WILL NEED

- **an adult**
- **limewater (obtain from school, science store, or science supply house)**
- **2 small flasks**
- **2 two-hole rubber stoppers**
- **4 glass tubes with right angle bends**
- **stopwatch or watch with a second hand**
- **notebook**
- **pen or pencil**

1. **Ask an adult** to insert the glass tubes with right angle bends into the holes in two 2-hole rubber stoppers (Figure 27a). Rubbing a drop of glycerin or soapy water on the tubes will allow them to pass through the holes more easily.

2. Place 100 mL of limewater in each of the two small flasks.

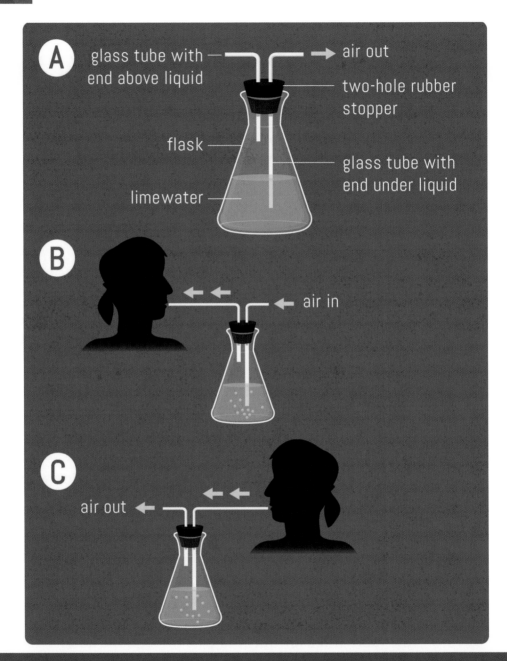

Figure 27. a) Limewater is placed in two flasks (only one is shown). Two stoppers, each with two right-angle glass tubes, are inserted into the flasks. b) In one flask, inhale air through your mouth from the shorter tube so that air has to pass through the longer tube and the limewater before reaching your mouth. c) Through the longer tube in the second flask, exhale the same air you inhaled. That exhaled air will also pass though the limewater.

3. Insert the rubber stoppers with the glass tubes into the mouths of the flasks.

4. Note and record the time in a notebook.

5. Put your lips around the shorter tube of one flask as shown in Figure 27b. Inhale a normal breath of air through your mouth. **(Caution: make sure you use the short straw and do not swallow the limewater! It is not safe for consumption.)**

    Notice that the air you inhale must pass through the limewater before reaching your mouth.

6. Exhale air through the tube that has its end below the limewater in the second flask as shown in Figure 27c. The expired air will also pass through the limewater.

7. Continue to inhale and exhale air in this way. In which flask does the limewater turn milky first? How long did it take?

8. Continue to inhale and exhale air through the limewater until the limewater in the other flask turns milky. How long did that take?

    The concentration of carbon dioxide in the air you inhale is about 0.04 percent. Based on your data, estimate the concentration of carbon dioxide in the air you exhale.

CHAPTER SIX

EXPLORING REAL TISSUE AND BONE

Part of a doctor's education includes dissections. One lengthy experiment during medical school is the dissection of a cadaver. A cadaver is a body that has been donated to science for study and research purposes. Doctors learn much about how the body works and how to treat it by studying cadavers. Many people have a will that states they want their body donated to a medical school. In that way, they can continue to contribute to medical education even after death.

EXPERIMENT 25

FINDING MUSCLES, BONES, TENDONS, AND OTHER TISSUES

You know there are bones, muscles, tendons, and ligaments in the human body. At this stage in your path to becoming a doctor, you can begin the first of many dissections by dissecting the wing of a chicken. Dissections are procedures of cutting open and studying plants and animals to explore further and understand their composition and function. You can find bones, muscles, tendons, and ligaments by looking beneath the skin of an uncooked chicken wing that you can buy at a grocery store. (Some schools have a course that gives students an opportunity to do dissections. If your school has such a course, be sure to enroll. The inside of a fetal pig, which you might dissect, is very similar to that of a tiny human being.)

THINGS YOU WILL NEED

- **an adult**
- **chicken wing**
- **newspapers**
- **sharp knife**
- **tweezers**
- **scissors (small and sharp work best)**
- **probe such as a slender stick or finishing nail**
- **paper towels**
- **garbage container**

1. Put the chicken wing on a thick layer of newspapers. **Ask an adult to help you cut it apart** so you can see the different tissues for yourself. You will need a sharp knife, a pair of tweezers, scissors, and a probe to pull, separate, and cut tissues. You'll also need paper towels to wipe your hands and instruments.

2. Most of the skin covering the wing can be pulled away with your fingers. You'll see a fatty layer attached to the skin. As you pull the skin off, look for connective tissue that attaches the skin to the muscles that lie under it.

3. The flesh beneath the skin and fat is mostly muscle. Notice how each muscle is covered by a very thin transparent membrane. Use tweezers and a probe, such as a stick or finishing nail, to separate the muscles from one another. See if you can find the origin and insertion of several of the muscles.

4. Find the tough, white, fibrous tendons that connect the muscles to bone. Use scissors to cut the tendons and remove the muscles to expose the bones.

5. The major bones in the wing are very similar to your arm bones. Can you find the humerus? Can you find the radius and ulna? How do the carpals, metacarpals, and phalanges of a chicken differ from yours?

6. Find the wide, tough, white ligaments that connect the humerus to the radius and ulna bones. Using scissors, cut through the ligaments that join these bones.

7. Examine the ends of the bones. Notice the glistening white cartilage covering the ends of the bones. What is the function of this cartilage? Can you find pads of yellow fat within the joint?

8. **Under adult supervision**, cut away all the tissue along the bones. Place the tissue on a paper towel. Wrap the tissue in the towel or towels and put it in a garbage container.

9. Set the bones aside to dry in a warm, safe place. You will use them in the next experiment.

10. **Wash your hands and work area thoroughly** with soap and warm water when you have finished working with the chicken wing. Raw chicken may contain bacteria that can make you sick.

EXPERIMENT 26

A LOOK INSIDE BONES

In this experiment, you'll examine more closely the bones you removed from the chicken wing.

THINGS YOU WILL NEED

- **bones from the chicken wing you dissected**
- **jar**
- **vinegar**
- **newspapers**
- **an adult**
- **knife**
- **hacksaw**
- **2 long beef bones**

1. Put the dry humerus bone you saved from the previous experiment in a jar of vinegar. Does the bone sink or float? What does this tell you about the density of chicken bone? Do you think the bone of a seagull would be more or less dense than a chicken bone? What makes you think so?

2. Put a cover on the jar. Leave the other dry bones beside the jar. Vinegar is an acid. It will slowly dissolve the minerals in bone. These minerals, mostly calcium and phosphorus plus small amounts of magnesium and sodium bicarbonate, constitute about two-thirds of a bone's weight. Organic matter—bone and cartilage cells and blood vessels—make up the remaining third.

3. After several days, remove the bone from the vinegar.
   How does its flexibility compare with that of the dry bones you left beside the jar?

4. The soft, flexible, plasticlike material that remains after the minerals have been removed would eventually decay if buried in soil. Under proper conditions, the mineral or hard part of bones might be preserved as a fossil.

5. Place the bone that you have soaked in vinegar on some newspapers. **Ask an adult** to use a sharp knife to cut the bone in half along its long axis to make what is called a longitudinal section.

6. Now you can see what is inside the bone. It will partly resemble the drawing in Figure 28, which shows a longitudinal section of a human long bone. The dense, or compact, bony tissue is found along the outside of the bone and makes up the shaft of long bones. The spongy (cancellous) bony tissue is found inside the shaft and especially near the ends of a bone. The medullary cavity runs along the central

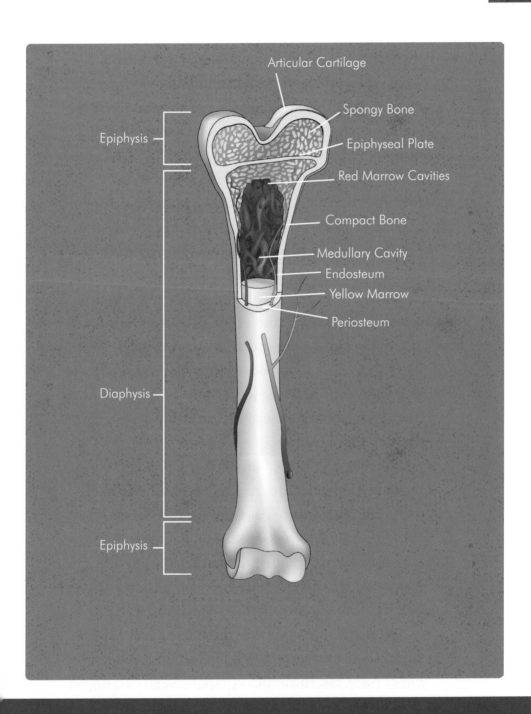

Figure 28. A drawing of a longitudinal section of a long bone (a tibia) shows the various tissues in the bone.

shaft of a long bone. It contains yellow marrow, which is mostly fatty tissue, and blood vessels. Red marrow, which is found near the ends of long bones, contains cells known as erythroblasts. Erythroblasts produce red blood cells.

Red blood cells contain hemoglobin. Hemoglobin is a chemical containing iron that combines with oxygen. So red blood cells are the cells that transport oxygen from your lungs to the cells of your body.

Except for their cartilaginous ends, bones are covered by a membrane called periosteum. The epiphysis is the wide end of a long bone. The diaphysis constitutes most of the bone's length. The wide ends give the joints greater stability. They reduce the pressure by spreading any force over a wider area.

7. After seeing the longitudinal section of a chicken bone, predict what the cross section will look like. Then **ask the adult** to cut across one of the *unsoftened* bones with a hacksaw. Does the cross section look the way you thought it would?

8. If possible, obtain two long beef bones from a butcher. The butcher might even cut one of them longitudinally for you. If not, **ask the adult** to use a hacksaw to make a longitudinal section of one bone. Also, **ask the adult** to make several cuts across the other bone. How do the longitudinal and cross

sections of the beef bones compare with those of the chicken bones? Does the medullary canal of the beef bone extend all the way into the epiphysis?

EXPLORING ON YOUR OWN

- Design and do an experiment to compare the densities of chicken and beef bones. Are the results what you would expect? If so, why? If not, why not?
- What foods must you eat to supply the minerals needed to make bone?
- Paleontologists have found broken animal bones near fossils believed to be species that preceded modern humans (*Homo sapiens*). They believe the bones were broken to obtain the marrow inside. Why would these precursors of humans want bone marrow?

A PARTING THOUGHT

The road to a medical degree (MD or DO) is long and steep, but the rewards are great. If you find you are still interested, we hope you will pursue that career or another one related to medicine, such as physician's assistant, nurse practitioner, nurse, pharmacist, or medical technician. All are worthwhile, needed, and desirable careers!

You will work with intelligent and capable colleagues, and you will have an opportunity to provide a much needed service to humanity. Saving lives, returning patients to good health after illness, curing diseases, eliminating disabilities, dealing with medical emergencies and trauma, even helping people cope with death are some of the greatest professional rewards available to a capable and competent human.

Finally, remember that patients respond best to a physician who is friendly, is kind, and has a sense of humor, as well as an ability to cure an illness, relieve pain, or remove an appendix.

GLOSSARY

alveoli—Little cavities, pits, or cells. In biology, it often refers to small sacs of air in the lungs.

arteries—Blood vessels that convey blood from the heart to the other parts of the body.

atria—The two upper chambers on each side of the heart. The atria take in blood from the veins and force it into the ventricles.

blood pressure—The pressure of blood against the inner walls of the blood vessels, measured using a sphygmomanometer.

capillaries—Tiny blood vessels connecting arteries to veins.

cartilage—Firm, whitish, flexible connective tissue found in various parts of the human body, such as the external ear and in the structure of joints.

center of mass—The point where the entire mass of a body may be considered to be concentrated.

diaphragm—The partition that separates the thoracic cavity from the abdominal cavity.

involuntary muscles—Any of the smooth muscles, except the cardiac muscle, that a being is not able to control by will.

joint—A place where two bones or elements of a skeleton join.

ligaments—Bands of tissue, usually white and fibrous that help to hold elements of a body together; specifically, ligaments connect bones.

sphygmomanometer—An instrument used to measure blood pressure in an artery. In a doctor's office, it is usually an inflatable cuff used with a stethoscope.

tendons—Cords or bands of dense, tough, inflexible tissue that connect a muscle to a bone part.

veins—Branching vessels or tubes that carry blood from various parts of the body to the heart.

ventricles—The two lower chambers on each side of the heart that receive blood from the atria. The blood is then forced into the arteries.

voluntary muscles—Muscles that are mainly controlled by a person's will; mostly the skeletal muscles.

FURTHER READING

BOOKS

Barnes-Svarney, Patricia. *The Handy Anatomy Answer Book*. Detroit, MI: Visible Ink Press, 2016.

Butterfield, Moira. *Amazing Body*. New York, NY: Little Bee Books, 2015.

Gawande, Atul. *Better: A Surgeon's Notes on Performance*. New York, NY: Picador. 2008.

Parker, Steve. *A Journey Through the Human Body*. Irvine, CA: QEB Publishing, Inc., 2015.

Reilly, Kathleen. *The Human Body: 25 Fantastic Projects Illuminate How the Body Works*. White River Junction, VT: Nomad Press, 2008.

Wicks, Maris. *Human Body Theater*. New York, NY: First Second, 2015.

Woodman, David, and Gerald Tharp. *Experiments in Physiology*. New York, NY: Pearson Publishing. 2014.

WEBSITES

AAMC

students-residents.aamc.org/choosing-medical-career/
    medical-careers/aspiring-docs/

A great resource for aspiring doctors.

Master's in Data Science

mastersindatascience.org/blog/the-ultimate-stem-guide-for-kids
    -239-cool-sites-about-science-technology-engineering-and
    -math/

Over 200 STEM links, including challenges and contests.

MIT Open Courseware

ocw.mit.edu/high-school/

MIT's open resources for high school students interested in
    a medical career.

Prospective Doctor

prospectivedoctor.com

A wide array of links for prospective doctors.

CAREER INFORMATION

BOOKS

Freedman, Jessica, MD. *The Medical School Interview: From Preparation to Thank You Notes.* New York, NY: MedEdits, 2010.

Freeman, Brian. *The Ultimate Guide to Choosing a Medical Specialty.* Columbus, OH: McGraw-Hill Education, 2013.

Goldberg, Edward M. *So, You Want to Be a Physician: Getting an Edge in Your Pursuit of the Challenging Dream of Becoming a Medical Professional.* CreateSpace Independent Publishing Platform, 2013.

Lee, Richard, MD. *Get Directions: A Career as a Physician: A Road Map for a Successful Career Begins in High School but Can Start from Anywhere.* Get Directions Publishing LLC, 2014.

WEBSITES

Big Future
bigfuture.collegeboard.org/majors-careers
A career and job website that focuses on college majors.

Explore Health Careers

explorehealthcareers.org

A great resource for those interested in a medical career.

Salary.com

*www1.salary.com/Healthcare-industry-Healthcare
-Practitioners-Salaries.html*

Description of salary expectations for various kinds of doctors, with links and descriptions.

Science Pioneers

sciencepioneers.org/students/stem-websites

Links to various STEM career websites.

INDEX